THE MERRYDOWN BOOK
OF
COUNTRY WINES

The Merrydown Book of Country Wines
André Launay

NEL

THE NEW ENGLISH LIBRARY

NEL Books are published by The New English Library Limited from Barnard's Inn, Holborn, London E.C.1. Made and printed in Great Britain by Hunt Barnard & Co. Ltd., Aylesbury, Bucks.

45000002 8

Contents

There is more rubbish talked about wine and wine tasting than anything else. It is the perfect subject for the snob, the one-up man, the bore and, because the true experts are patient and polite people who prefer drinking wines to talking about them, only the views of the amateur are expressed and they become more and more banal as time goes on.

To sample a few wines with a professional 'sommelier' in the cellars of a restaurant is one thing, to listen to the conversation of amateur wine-men during a 'wine tasting' is another.

"Extravagant would you say?"

"Lusty."

"Lusty? Perhaps. An unmistakable mood of flippancy."

"I think it's undisciplined."

"It's a bit disobedient, one must admit."

"Naughty. Just naughty. It's a naughty little wine."

On more than one occasion I have decanted a rather lousy Algerian into a Lynch-Bages bottle and watched my guests go into raptures over its 'bouquet', and once I went as far as doctoring a glass of Spanish Graves with half a tablet of Alka-Seltzer when I couldn't afford Champagne—promised to a particularly delectable red-head. No one ever knew.

Recently, however, a similar trick was played on me from which, I am delighted to say, I have greatly profited.

I was dining with a friend in Paris and he offered, with

the Pate de Foie Gras, a white wine which he served from a decanter into a tall coloured glass one usually associates with Rhine wines.

It was very pale, very clear, clean and white and I decided that it was a Riesling. It turned out to be an English wine made from white currants.

This revelation was followed by a lecture from my friend on the lack of adventure in the English palate.

"They allow themselves to believe what they are told, he said, "And as they have been told that French wines are the best and that there are no English wines, they have never seriously tried to make their own."

> Bon Français, quand je vois mon verre
> Plein de couleur de feu,
> Je songe, en remerciant Dieu,
> Qu'ils n'ent ont pas en Angleterre.

The translation of which is :-

> Good Frenchman, when I see my glass
> Full of fiery coloured wine,
> I muse, and thank the Lord,
> That they have none in England.

"This of course is simply not true. They have wine in England in abundance if they wish, it is just a matter of making it and telling the natives that just because dear old spinsters in innocent rose-covered cottages brew it in their garden sheds it doesn't mean to say that it is a joke. The dear old English spinster, in fact, has been living it up a good deal more than many a beer drinker for years."

Fired by this noble Frenchman's enthusiasm, I returned to England and searched for English wines.

I was surprised to find that some are marketed, like

French wines, labelled and in bottles—and really are extraordinarily good.

I believe that the English wines have many qualities that French wines do not have, and though I would not go as far as saying that they are better—they are comparable and certainly ideal for everyday drinking.

In the pages that follow I have collected together all the information I have learned about English wines. I hope to enlighten those who, like myself, are curious to know more about the subject, and I hope to make it clear to the average wine drinker in this country that it is really only centuries of clever propaganda by the French that has given the English wine maker an inferiority complex about his product.

1

A Brief History of Wines
in England

A BRIEF HISTORY OF WINES IN ENGLAND

The first step that man took away from the life of the beast was in the making of fire. The second step was in brewing.

The malting of grains is such a complicated process that one would imagine it to be the product of an advanced mind, but the earliest records of man give evidence that he was busy making beer and making wine. As soon as he could scrawl on walls, in fact, he did so in the praise of alcoholic beverages.

Grape wine has enjoyed more attention in recorded history than any other drink and its existence can be traced back some 10,000 years. Proof has been found that man was making wine in Asia Minor during the Tertiary period. Early Egyptian history records that Byblos was very famous for wine, and it is generally agreed that it was the Greeks in the first millenium B.C. who introduced the vine to Italy and Southern France.

Wine was brought to England during the Roman occupation and vines were grown under the Governorship of Agricola in 78 A.D.

The emperor Domitian (81-96 A.D.) later, however, decreed that all vines should be uprooted beyond the borders of Italy, so that there would be no competition in the commercial field of wine selling.

Though it is doubtful whether this order was carried out, no new vines were planted in this country till 280 A.D. when the emperor Probus permitted vines to be grown again in Gaul, Spain and Britain.

The first successful vineyard was planted at Vine in Hampshire and historians have presumed that small vineyards were cultivated wherever there was a Roman villa, though not much evidence of this is available due to the fact that the period between the end of the third century and early Saxon times is, historically, poorly documented.

The first reliable post-Roman trace of wine can be found in the Venerable Bede's Ecclesiastical History of England which he wrote in 734. In it he says:-

"Britain excels for grain and trees, and is well
adapted for feeding cattle and beasts of burden.
It also produces vines in some places, and has plenty
of land and water-fowls of several sorts; it is
remarkable also for rivers abounding in fish, and
plentiful springs."

Vines are later mentioned by Alfred the Great who legislated for vineyard as property. In his laws are found:-

"Compensation shall be paid at an exact valuation
by anyone damaging the vineyard or field of another"

King Edwy, King Alfred's grandson, granted the vineyard of Pathensburgh in Somerset to the monks of Glastonbury in 955, and in the Domesday book 38 vineyards are mentioned, some of which were found at Bitesham in Berkshire, Chenetone in Middlesex, Hantum in Worcestershire, Holbourne in Middlesex, Ware in Hertfordshire, Westminster, and Wilcote in Wiltshire.

In 1125 William of Malmesbury wrote about Gloucestershire,
"The county is planted more thickly with vineyards than any other in England, more plentiful in crops and more pleasant in flavour. For the wines do not offend the mouth with sharpness since they do not yield to the French sweetness."

Though vine growing and wine making was popular in the 12th century and after, it never flourished as a business. There were better and quicker ways of making money than by cultivating the vine and in 1152 a historical event started the steep decline of viticulture—Henry Plantagenet of Anjou married Eleanor of Aquitaine. As part of her dowry he obtained a large piece of South West France, including the ancient port of Bordeaux.

Two years later Henry became King of England and with his accession to the throne the whole of his overseas possessions—which with the addition of Aquitaine represented half of France—became part of England. Wine ships from Bordeaux started sailing to this country to unload their cargoes of barrels at the ports of Southern England and this state of affairs lasted for the next three hundred years.

The long period of unrestricted wine importation left its mark for ever on the English palate. Only when the gradual evacuation of France in the 15th century took place did the wine trade begin to diminish, but by then the English had more than developed their taste for claret and had long forgotten about their own viticulture.

Though the loss of the French territories resulted in

15

more expensive wines, making it less available except to the very rich, viticulture itself did not develop. Interest instead turned to the making of wines in the home with other fruit.

Beer was brewed quarterly in cottages and once a month in the richer houses. Fruit wines were made as each ingredient came into season and such wines became an important part of the household pharmacopœia, their medicinal qualities understood and highly appreciated. Celery wine was used against gout and rheumatism, Cowslip an antidote for insomnia. Elderberry wine was a remedy against coughs and colds in winter, Herb wines a carminative, and Parsnip wine respected as a laxative.

The knowledge of baking and brewing became an essential part of a girl's education. As wives they were in charge of those duties except in households where the husband liked looking after the business of brewing. Certain men and women gained local fame for their wines and beers and many inns and ale houses relied on the ability of the proprietors for their success.

The Elizabethan housewife made wine far more commonly than she made jam. Jam was for children, an indulgence, like sweets.

Until the middle of the 17th century everyone drank home-made wines for even the richest people could not live in splendour all the time. Life was a matter of enjoying while you could and enduring when you had to. Before modern methods of farming and refrigeration guaranteed the same quantity of food all the year round, there had to be periods of rigorous fasting for everybody, the food was just not there. Lords and ladies ate pottage and drank country wines along with their humblest servants. When an ox was killed and its consumption purely domestic and a personal matter, it was not slaughtered lightly. Swans and peacocks were luxuries even to the wealthiest, and the great butts of French, Spanish and Portuguese wines that were imported and brought to the manor houses and castles by horse and cart were not opened frivolously. The staple diets were bread, bacon pottage, beans, mutton and venison, beer, cider, mead and other home-made fruit wines.

When Charles II was restored to the throne in 1660, however, things started changing. The court was influenced by the French way of life and delighted in having little respect for English ideas and customs and a definite dislike for country life. With Charles II came the notion that the aristocracy were a class privileged to do nothing at all but amuse themselves all day, and the city was the place to be amused in.

By the beginning of the 17th century it was considered smart and amusing for a lady to say "I loathe the country and everything that relates to it. I nauseate while walking."

The still room was the first department of the manor house to suffer the consequences of this trend. The ladies now spent the "season" in London which happened to coincide with the season of most activity in the country. When they returned to their country houses it was no longer to brew and bake, but to dawdle in the gardens and play cards. At the sight of mere rustics they would have the "vapours" and the local inhabitants were referred to as "Boars", "Toads" and "Hogsnorton squires in boots".

Home-brewed wines were naturally no longer quite good enough for their delicate tastes. Port and Claret were the only suitable drinks for the gentlemen and while they drank themselves into a stupor the ladies consoled themselves by tippling gin bought in fancy bottles and labelled "Cuckolds Comfort" or "Ladies Delight".

The custom of home brewing however did not die down. The middle classes still carried on well into the 19th century. Jane Austen (1775-1817) in a letter to her sister

Cassandra inquired about the state of the various home brews. Writing from her rich brother's house, Godnersham Park, she begged her sister not to imagine that she was spoilt by the drinking of French wines every day. The Austens made orange wine, mead, currant wines and spruce beer.

The first real change in tradition affecting the middle class drinking customs came with the arrival of tea. When it was first introduced into England it was brought overland, on caravan routes across Asia from China. The cost was prohibitive till the East India Company started planting tea in India and shipped it over at lower prices.

Though cheaper, it was still too expensive to become the common drink it is to-day, till the clipper ships came into service. Then in one generation tea drinking ousted beer drinking.

The "tea set" of those days however came up against some pretty fierce opposition. Tea was evil. Reformers raged and public-spirited men and women did all in their power to combat this awful new drink which lacked food value and was still more expensive than the good, wholesome, strengthening beer. Labourers who drank it were warned that they would soon be useless and lose all their initiative. William Cobbet in his "Cottage Economy" denounced tea as a poison and encouraged the brewing and drinking of stronger beverages, but to no avail. Tea won the day—wine became cheaper and more popular and, slowly but surely, home-made English wines declined till to-day the custom of offering a glass of home-made brew with a piece of home-made biscuit is looked upon as quite quaint and endearingly amusing.

2

The Grape Vine in England

THE GRAPE VINE IN ENGLAND

There is no reason, other than an economic one, why England should not produce its own wine from its own grapes. It is not a question of the country's unsuitability, for history records that England *was* a vine growing country, it is simply that it could never, now, start a big enough production to compete with all that is made on the Continent.

Before Henry Plantagenet caused the mass of importation of Bordeaux wines by his marriage, Worcestershire was the most famous county for viticulture. In the Twelfth and Thirteenth centuries its vineyards were more important than its fruit orchards are to-day. Worcestershire Priory had a vineyard at Fladbury and there were others at Grimlaye and Droitwich until the 1250s.

In the parish of Cotteridge there were four large vineyards one of which lasted for three centuries. At Hampton in the vale of Evesham monks cultivated the vine on a terraced side of the hill. This vineyard was planted in 1084.

Vines also flourished at Abberton as late as 1554 and were under cultivation at Allesborough Hill, Brushley, Leigh and Seven Stoke.

According to documents Henry III thought the best grapes grown in England in his time came from Hailing in East Kent, but Lincolnshire was also famous for its vineyards—the centre of the growing area being Ely.

In London the site of Holborn vineyard is commemorated by the name of Vine Street and it is more than likely that any street bearing that name indicates that once there was a vineyard on the site.

In the Middle Ages every monastery had its own vineyard but it is in Henry VIII's time, during the dissolution of the monasteries that viticulture on a large scale took a steep decline. The rise in the wealth of the class whose fortunes were founded directly, or indirectly, on Church property, came to a halt and fewer men were now willing to risk investment in the English vine when it was already proving more profitable to concentrate on the buying, shipping and selling of foreign wine.

In Charles II's time there was, however, sufficient interest in the making of grape wine for John Rose, the king's gardener, to write a book with the help of John Evelyn, the diarist, called THE ENGLISH VINEYARD VINDICATED. In it he stated that vines liked poor soil as much as brambles. He was in charge of the Royal vineyard.

James II had vineyards at Oatlands in Surrey. Sir Robert Cecil, the 1st Earl of Salisbury, planted thirty thousand plants at Hatfield. Later Sir William Temple brought some new varieties from France and another wrote a paper on a certain Colonel Blunt's vineyard at Blackheath. Vineyards were not at all uncommon. In the 18th century Brandy was made from the grapes grown at Beaulieu Abbey, more vines were grown successfully in Chelsea,

Wimbledon and Rotherhithe. In his book ICHNO-
GRAPHIA RUSTICA, published in 1742, one Stephen
Switzer wrote that. . . .

"Vineyards may be so cultivated in England, as to
produce large quantities of grapes, and those so well
ripened, as to afford a good and substantial vinous
juice, needs no demonstration; when in the various parts
of Somersetshire there are, at the time, flourishing
vineyards, and the vineyard of the late Sir William
Basset has annually produced some hogsheads of good
bodied and palatable wine, which I have been credibly
informed by Gentlemen who have drunk considerable
quantities of it with great satisfaction."

In another book, TREATISE ON THE VINE OR
GRAPE TREE, a certain Bartholomew Roque is recorded
in 1790, as having had a vineyard in Waltham Green for
over thirty years, in a common field which, though flat,
produced wine as good as that of Orleans and Auxerre.

In THE COMPLEAT TREATISE OF PRACTICAL
HUSBANDRY, the author, Dr Hales, wrote that in Bath
three vineyards had been worked for profit by a farmer
and that. . . .

"I have drunk with the distinguished and eminent Dr
Shaw wines made under his own care from a little
vineyard behind his own garden in Kensington which
equal many of the lighter wines of France; and while
good care was taken of the vineyard at Hammersmith,
a great deal of very good wine was obtained for sale,
though neither of these were favourable plots."

At Pains Hill in Surrey a viticulturist had a vineyard on
the South side of a gentle hill with gravelly soil. In it he
planted two sorts of Burgundy grapes, Auverbat and Pinot
Meunier. The first year a red wine was made, but it was

23

harsh. He then tried pressing the grapes instead of treading them and this resulted in a white wine that was so good that it tasted like Champagne. After a few years he was making a really very good wine which sparkled and he sold it to wine merchants for fifty guineas a hogshead. One wine merchant sold £500 worth at one time in 7/6 and 10/– bottles but even then the prejudice of most people against anything of English growth was such that he found it more prudent not to declare where the vines grew until they had passed their verdict on it.

It was generally admitted that the English climate did not help the cultivation of the vine and that many crops were spoiled by May frosts and wet summers. Though these Champagne type wines were an undoubted success no one took the risk of investing well in a possible English wine till 1875 when an expert viticulturist, Mr Pettigrew, planted a large vineyard at Castle Coch in Glamorganshire on the lands belonging to the Marquess of Bute.

The variety he planted there—less than a hundred years ago—were of the Gamay Noire type which yielded a successful wine which was sold in great quantities. Under the same patronage he planted a nine acre vineyard at Swanbridge a little later and this yielded over 2,000 gallons of wine, about 12,000 bottles. This would in time have doubled, it usually takes eight years for vines to give their peak crops, but the project was thwarted by the 1914 war which put an end to the cultivation. No more was done in England on a commercial scale till 1945 when two now famous viticulturists, Mr R. Barrington Brock and Mr Edward Hyams set about the problems of experimenting with the grape at a specially set up Viticultural Research Station at Oxted in Surrey.

To be successful, wine growing in England needs great care. It is not agriculture but horticulture, the difference between farming and gardening. Possibly for reasons of

24

climate the English are not naturally wine drinking people but beer and spirit drinkers, so the interest in the vine has never been very overwhelming, but if the 17th century capitalists had not imported foreign wines and had concentrated their money and efforts in vine growing at home it is more than likely that the sunny slopes of Cornwall, Gloucestershire, Worcestershire and Essex would now be covered with vineyards and wine snobs would be discussing the qualities of a Chateau Berkeley '64 and imbibing an acceptable Chateau Canterbury '62.

Any climate that ripens apples will ripen certain varieties of grapes. The main climatic need for the vine is a warm, dry autumn. The vine is a temperate zone plant, but certain varieties are grown both north and south of this zone. In the case of northern cultivations shelter from cold winds is as essential as catching the sun. In the south shelter from the sun is needed, however. During the dormant period the vine is remarkably tough and can stand quite a bit of cold. The Champagne vineyards, for instance, are often covered with snow, the vines are protected by ploughing soil over the stock. But cold is in fact necessary.

Severe winters check the growth of plants allowing more abundant fruiting to take place later. Frosts are not fatal.

A hundred years ago vines in Europe were grown on their own roots and propagated by cuttings and layers. This is no longer so on the Continent due to the phylloxera epidemic.

The pyhlloxera is an insect which lives on the American vine where it forms small galls and normally does not affect the plant, but in 1870 it found its way to Europe and for some reason started living off the roots and leaves killing the vine. This was a disaster, and thousands of acres of vineyards in France were ruined.

An American entomologist eventually discovered that the American root was resistant to the insect and that by grafting the good fruit of the European vines on to the roots of the American plant the problem could be overcome.

In England, however, this has not yet proved necessary. as the phylloxera does not exist on this side of the Channel. Great care must be taken though that anyone bringing over the continental vines does not also bring over the dreaded insect.

There are, of course, many varieties of grape vines. Those that grow in England in many of the gardens of old mansions in Kent, Surrey, and Hampshire have vines to which it is difficult to assign names, but it is generally accepted that to grow new vine cuttings from these old ones are the best to use. Black Hamburgh, Gamay Hatif des Vosges, Brandt for black grapes, Royal Muscadine, Madeleine Royale and S. 1990 for white have proved successful also.

Grapes will grow in almost any soil and they have the advantage that the poorer the ground the better the wine. Though less fruit will grow.

Vines can be grown either against walls or in open ground. Against walls they will thrive in the northern and colder regions. Right in the centre of the West End of London in Stratford Place a magnificent grape vine still grows up from the basement. It is the only bit of greenery for some distance around and was planted over a hundred years ago by the Dowager Lady Ellanborough, who put a clause in the selling contract of the house that the vine should always be cared for. The house now belongs to Coty.

The best exposure for a wall grape is facing south east or south. A south facing wall has the obvious advantage of getting more sun in the autumn when it is necessary to ripen the grapes well and raise their sugar content.

Interest in vine growing is greatly increasing now with more people going on the continent and enjoying wine. Amateur growers all over the country are experimenting in back gardens, and in some quarters wine production is shaping so well that a number of growers have got together to form the English Vineyards Association. This Association already has over fifty members, sixteen of whom are owners of producing vineyards, two of whom have enough to produce on a commercial scale.

Hampshire at present seems to be the "in" place for wine production with large vineyards at Beaulieu and Hambledon.

3

Grape Wines and Fruit Wines

GRAPE WINES AND FRUIT WINES

Wine is the fermented, cleared and matured drink made from fruit. Generally it applies to the drink made only from the grape and because in France wine, by law, must be the product solely made from grapes, some people believe to call alcoholic drinks made from other fruit 'wine' is a misnomer. It is not in fact so. The fermented, cleared, and matured juice of any fruit, be it apricot, bilberry, red or white currant or grape is wine. Of all the fruits, however, the grape is the most suitable for making wine having the highest sugar content.

In young fruit the glucose and acids begin to form together with water. Under the influence of the sun and heat the acid decreases and the sugar content increases. A number of other substances are also present, tartrates, gums, oils and tannin in the skin (as far as grapes are concerned) but the main products of fruit growth are sugar, acid and water.

In fruit wine all these substances play an important part. The sugar becomes alcohol, the acids produce the taste, the other complex compounds add the special flavours and scents.

There is little difference between the making of grape wines and fruit wines, both of which can be made from ameliorated must—from juices which are not quite up to standard and have to have sugar or acids added, and often a little water when the acid content is too high.

To make apple wine, for instance, sugar must be added to provide adequate alcohol. The acid content is usually well balanced, but in the case of other fruit it is often in excess with the exception of pears which have too little. The more acid fruits have to have water added so that their acidity does not overpower the flavour and the resultant sugar content reduction must be compensated. Additional sugar is converted into alcohol and does not necessarily make the drink sweeter. Many people who have never tried fruit wines are under the impression that they not only taste of the fruit they were made from, but are also very sweet. This is very far from the truth.

Due to the necessity of ameliorating fruit wines, of adding sugar and reducing acids in the right amounts, it is far easier to make wine from grapes than from other fruit. Anyone can do this without difficulty but the technical knowledge required in order to achieve a balanced wine from fruits which for centuries have been regarded as totally unsuited for this purpose cannot be acquired in a day.

Considerable alterations can occur both in the flavour and appearance of wine during its protracted existence in cask and bottle. This is easy to understand if one remembers that it is not an artificial liquid but a living organism, irrevocably associated with the soil, and therefore bound to behave like other forms of plant life that have undergone preservative treatment.

The preservation of fruit juice caused by the spontaneous conversion of sugar into alcohol, bottling and other refinements of cellar technique, is simply a process of arrested development accomplished for the benefit of mankind. Although the forces of Nature have been inhibited by alcoholic fermentation, alterations will take place anyway. Although alcohol will prevent the activities of unwelcome micro-organisms such as those generally associated with the decay of rotting fruit, it will do little to interfere with the normal process of maturing.

One of the biological changes affecting wines made from ANY KIND OF FRUIT, is caused by what is known as oxidation. This phenomenon can best be observed by cutting an apple in half. The flesh at first appears white, but after a few minutes begins to change colour, passing from yellow to dull brown. If the apples are pressed the extracted juice will behave in the same way, although the process of darkening will take much longer. Even if the juice is converted into cider by fermentation or from cider to cider-vinegar, the browning will not be prevented from taking place, nor will it be avoided by keeping the liquid from the air by sealing in a bottle.

Apples are not the only fruit to be affected in this way; exactly the same kind of discolouration will occur in grape wine unless adequate steps are taken to prevent it. Unfortunately the change in colour is accompanied by a disagreeable deterioration of flavour, particularly in the case of white wines, a notable exception being found in the case of sherry, where oxidation is encouraged by a special process, so that the wine may acquire its characteristic and individual flavour.

It is a fallacy to suggest that a dark brown cider is in any way more potent than one with a delicate amber hue; the strength depends entirely on the alcohol content and the alcohol has nothing to do with colour. The browning of a white wine or cider in fact, indicates neglect or carelessness on the part of the manufacturer for there exists a perfectly good method of preventing its occurrence.

Oxidation is caused by an enzyme, a variety of oxidase, which causes oxygen to combine with astringent compounds of the fruit, notably tannin. Both white and red wines are affected by this troublesome development. Ciders are particularly vulnerable, for sufficient soluble oxygen is always present in the liquid to provide the conditions necessary for further evolution.

The occurrence of this seems to be more frequent in wines produced from over-ripe or damaged fruit.

Oxidation enzymes can, however, be destroyed by pasteurisation. The liquid is heated, maintained at a high temperature for a brief period, then cooled rapidly. This is common practice in the production of non-alcoholic fruit juices, but many vintners prefer to use other methods rather than subject their delicate liquids to any form of heat. The presence of a reducing agent such as ascorbic acid or sulphur dioxide deters the process of oxidation effectively, and both these chemical preservatives are used for that purpose in the beverage industry.

Sulphur dioxide has the advantage of putting a stop to any activity by undesirable micro-organisms and it is therefore used a great deal in the preparation of wine and cider. Liquids are usually impregnated with it, for sulphur dioxide is a gas obtained by burning sulphur in the presence of oxygen. Alternatively it can be introduced in the form of a salt—potassium metabisulphite—which generates the gas as it dissolves.

Fermentation is a wholly natural process which occurs spontaneously in fruit juice unless measures are taken to prevent it. Although naturally endowed with the correct organic ingredients, fruit juice is by no means the only medium which can support this important physiological

34

metamorphosis. It is fundamental to remember that fermentation is only a link in the complicated sequence of growth and decay and that the production of alcohol, valuable though it is, is purely a coincidence.

Fermentation is caused by the presence of certain micro-organisms known as saccharomyces or "sugar fungus". By becoming active in certain environments, these so-called yeast cells induce a form of enzyme known as zymase which converts sugar into almost equal parts of ethyl alcohol and carbon dioxide gas. As they do so they generate heat and cause a great deal of turbulence in the liquid. The duration of activity depends on a number of factors such as the vigour of the yeast, the temperature, the availability of nutrients and so on.

Spontaneous fermentation is difficult to stop. Among the many alcohol-forming yeasts which find their way into fermentable liquids there exist both vigorous and feeble varieties, any of which can multiply fast enough to dominate the fermentation.

Wild yeasts are likely to produce unsatisfactory results and it is up to the wine maker to eliminate the undesirable and introduce, if necessary, the strain of yeast which guarantees the maximum degree of efficiency.

A variety of pure yeast cultures are produced at viticulture and pomological research institutes which are capable of unimpaired activity in conditions usually considered to be unsuitable for natural development. As a consequence yeasts can be supplied which tolerate unusually low temperatures, high alcohol contents, excessive concentrations of tannin and overdoses of sulphur.

Promoting a healthy fermentation is one thing. Stopping its occurrence is another. The activity of yeast cells can be discouraged by high concentrations of sugar, sulphur dioxide or alcohol, by extremes of temperatures or atmospheric pressure and by lack of nitrogen. It can be completely eliminated by removing the yeast cells or destroying them.

The total removal of micro-organisms from a liquid can only be effectively achieved by intensive filtration, a complicated process involving the accurate sterilization of all equipment prior to use.

The stability of a wine or ordinary non-alcoholic fruit juice for retail is dependent partly on the efficiency with which these measures are carried out and partly on the possible incidence of re-infection, either due to inadequate sterilization of bottles, corks, casks and other containers, or by airborne contamination of the contents after the seal has been removed. Fruit juices are particularly susceptible to this trouble, unfortified sweet wines—such as moselles and hocks—to a lesser extent, due to the inhibitory action of the alcohol.

The alcoholic content of a beverage usually causes considerable confusion in most people's minds. The strength of a drink can never be accurately gauged by the palate—as has been recently disclosed by the breathalyser test experiments—or by the effect it may have on the sensory nerves. A reliable assessment of alcoholic content is therefore valuable specially in view of the fact that the cost of liquor is more than ever influenced by the amount of actual spirit it happens to contain.

With obstinate persistence Great Britain still maintains her own exclusive system of weights and measures, but when it comes to alcohol determination even other countries have not yet agreed to accept universal calculation based on the usual decimal system.

There are three principal methods of expressing and defining alcohol content. First, as a percentage by volume of absolute alcohol present. Second as a percentage by weight. Third as a percentage of proof spirit in degrees.

The first calculation is made according to Gay Lussac's

Scale which is recognized in France and Belgium, or sometimes according to the Tralles Scale which is used in Austria, Italy and Russia.

The Hydrometers involved are constructed so that they are accurate at temperatures of 59 and 60 degrees Fahrenheit respectively, and give readings which only differ by .2 degrees.

Alcohol expressed as a percentage by weight is the calculation officially accepted in Germany but, as in other countries, percentage by volume is generally agreed to be simpler to understand and more practical.

In England and the United States alcohol is measured in degrees or as a percentage of proof spirit, but the two scales do not correspond. This is because proof spirit in Great Britain contains 57% of alcohol volume, but in America only 50%.

This odd method of assessing spirit content originally arose from a quick and appropriate test designed to prove the quality of French brandies on arrival at British ports. If a small quantity of gunpowder, soaked in the liquid, was found to ignite satisfactorily, the brandy was considered to be up to standard. On the other hand if the gunpowder failed to ignite, it was assumed that the brandy had been watered down and so failed to stand up to the "proof".

Spirit found to pass this primitive test was said to be 100 degrees proof, but in fact consisted of 57.06 parts of pure alcohol and 42.94 parts of water. 100 per cent pure alcohol therefore is 175 degrees proof—which starts the confusion. Following on this, a liquor labelled 30 degrees *under proof* can be described as 70 degrees *proof*. Proof spirit is a percentage of a percentage of alcohol.

To convert degrees proof spirit into percentage alcohol volume it is necessary to multiply by 57 and divide by 100. To convert percentage by volume into degrees proof spirit it is necessary to multiply by 100 and divide by 57.

At the end of it all, however, it is not, in fact, the alcoholic content of a wine that makes it good. Those who wish to indulge in the effects of alcohol can do so by drinking spirits. Wine, sophisticated wine, is purchased by the consumer for its taste first, and its effect after.

A sophisticated wine might be described as one which has been adulterated or mixed with some foreign substance. The word has a meaning which implies that some kind of debasement has been allowed and, for that reason, may not altogether be acceptable, but sophistication is allowed to occur in the wine trade on a scale considerably larger than might be expected.

Wine is usually described as a product obtained exclusively by the fermentation of grapes in the presence, or absence, of their skins. The fruit must be completely fresh or only partially dried, such as might be achieved by allowing the berries to shrivel a little in the sun. The use of raisins is not permitted. This precise definition quite clearly excludes a number of alcoholic products popularly known as wine, thanks to additions made for the purpose of amelioration, or in the interests of general stability, the absence of which might create certain marketing problems.

Take Champagne, for instance. The carbon dioxide gas which provides the sparkle in this drink is not, in any way, an artificial or foreign substance. It is naturally produced by inducing a secondary fermentation in a sealed bottle. On the other hand, sugar is a material which was not present in the grapes from which the wine was made, nor was the sweetening syrup added to replace the unsightly deposit caused by fermentation which cannot be allowed to remain in the bottle, and must be forcibly removed by disgorgement.

Fortified wines fare no better under similar scrutiny. They comprise port, sherry, madeira, marsala, malaga, some Californian, Greek and Dominion wines, together with those from France, generally known as "vins doux naturels". All are exalted in alcohol content by the addition of spirit which, though it may often be obtained from grape juice, involves distillation, a process completely divorced from the natural conversion of sugar into alcohol and carbon dioxide by the action of yeast cells.

Vermouths are wines which have been fortified with spirit then flavoured by the addition of aromatic herbs. The most important of these is wormwood, from which the name is derived, but they include a number of others, such as gentian, coriander, centaury, calamus root, horehound and elder flowers, to mention but a few.

Nor are the common table wines quite exempt from criticism. Geographically the vineyards of Germany are on the viticulture fringe. Limited sunshine tends to produce wine with too much acid and too little sugar. To make them drinkable, such wines need to be ameliorated by the addition of sugar for the production of alcohol, with perhaps water or some neutralising chemical to reduce acidity. It is not fully appreciated but eighty per cent of German wines are subject to this sort of sophistication.

French wines produced north of Lyons and Bordeaux are tampered with in the same way. Wines from southern latitudes are correspondingly deficient in acid and cannot be marketed without undergoing some kind of adjustment.

Wine therefore, grape wine, continental wine, the wine of Bacchus which is respected and eulogized, is not all that pure nor perfect. Objections to the sophistications it undergoes may, however be considered trifling, in spite of the purists. Water constitutes the principal ingredient of most fruits and in the case of grape juice it amounts to between 84% and 92% of the whole. It can be argued that added water can never be as exquisitely pure as that contained in the fruit itself, but an objection based on a theory such as this is scarcely important enough to warrant attention.

On aesthetic grounds additions to fruit juice for the purpose of restoring sugar deficiency is also known to be an objection. This is done by blending the juice with an improved must of liberal sweetness, or by the direct addition of sugar itself. But sugar from either source will be converted into exactly the same ethyl alcohol and carbon dioxide by the process of fermentation.

In view of the fact that fruit wines undergo the same sophistication as grape wines, it is strange that in the minds of many the fruit wines are not considered as pure. They are, often, purer, not having to be subjected to quite so much tampering—but fruit wines, and English fruit wines especially, have to compete with four or five hundred years of intense publicity and praise for the grape.

4

Apple Wine, Cider, Mead and Country Wines

APPLE WINE, CIDER, MEAD AND COUNTRY WINES

APPLE WINE AND CIDER

Cider may well have been the first ever alcoholic drink to be tasted by man. The apple is certainly the very first fruit to be encountered by him on that fatal day when he also met woman in all her glory. Did Adam and Eve, once out of the Garden of Eden, make most of the fruit, drinking its juice, letting it ferment, drowning their lonely sorrows in the resulting intoxication? Such details were never recorded and must remain a supposition.

The first accounts of the apple come with stories handed down from the Druids. The apple and the oak were the only two trees on which the sacred mistletoe grew. The apple and the oak were therefore worshipped.

When Christianity, in its Celtic form, first came to England it was said to be established on the Island of Avalon. Avalon—the Island of Apples. It was a mount

used for ceremonial occasions by the Druids near Glastonbury, in Somerset. So apples were still in the running for
being a bit special, but after this period its sacred reputation got lost and since then it has just been regarded as a
rather ordinary common garden fruit.

The Romans brought various types of apples, sweeter
and juicier, from the Mediterranean, so they were possibly
responsible for its cultivation in England, like everything
else, but for once they don't really come into the History
of the English apple at all. In fact the apple is remarkably
poorly documented and apart from hints that libations of
cider were poured onto the ground at Twelfth Night, bob-
bing for apples was a custom at Hallowe'en and roasted
apples were put in Wassail bowls, little else is known.

No one seems to know, either, when cider was first
made. The ancient Greeks knew about it, the Romans had
a Latin word for it—Cisera—which became the French—
Cidre—and our own—Cider. In the "13th century chron-
icles of Charlemagne" a fermented drink with an apple base
is reported being made in Normandy, after which it is
accepted as an everyday drink, mentioned in songs and in
such drinking proverbs as:-

> Cider on Beer makes good Cheer;
> Beer on Cider makes a bad Rider.

Cider, in fact, is the cheapest way of getting a hang-
over.

It is a strong drink, producing an intoxication which
has something in common with some truth drugs. You feel
at one with the earth and very quickly aware of your own
insignificance. It produces memorable dreams, but if you
know how to drink it you can wake up with a clear head.
If you don't, you can experience the fiercest 'morning
after' imaginable.

Special apples are used for making cider, sweet, acid

and tart. They should be dry with a high tannin and sugar content.

Between September and October the cider orchards of Dorset, Devon, Hereford and Norfolk are picked, the apples shaken down in bulk, put into sacks and sent to the factories. They are poured into special baths and hosed down with clean water.

They are then cut up, squashed and reduced to a pulp which is spread on coarse cloth in layers. The presses then move up and down crushing the pulp and squeezing all the juice out of it. The juice is then collected and poured into vats where it is left to ferment for two or three weeks— the normal time it takes for the sugar to be converted into alcohol.

The resulting liquid is a rough, dry cider. This is then filtered to remove all sediment acquired during fermentation and sugar is added to make sweet cider. Others are blended to suit different palates, new juices added to old.

Bottled cider is chilled at 35 deg. F, and gas injected to make it sparkle. It is sweeter than draught cider and headier than bottled beer though the alcoholic content is usually the same. Four draught ciders are usually available, Dry, Medium, Medium-Sweet, Sweet, Sweet and Conditioned. Conditioned cider is known in the West country as Scrumpy, a name which covers a multitude of sins if made at home, but if manufactured means simply that a quantity of yeast has been added to each cask to produce further fermentation. It is much drier and more potent. In early winter newly-made cider is quite harmless, but the same cider drunk in the following summer can have a totally different effect.

The difference between sweet and dry ciders was once only a matter of the type of apple used, but now the old sweet cider is not considered sweet enough. Sugar and honey are added in some cases.

In England cider is customarily drunk at the strength the good fermentation of a natural apple juice yields, but there are many ways of producing a higher alcoholic content. Some French farmers make Calvados, a clear spirit, by boiling the must till it is reduced by half and then fermenting the liquor which turns into a very fiery drink. For some reason such drinks are not very popular in this country and from the apple more gentle beverages are made. Apple wine, for instance, a light, agreeable, thirst quenching drink which is quite alcoholic enough for most people.

Cider and apple wine are also valued by country people for their medicinal properties, they act against rheumatism it is said, but only if the cider is very dry, the adding of a sweetener nullifying the effect.

Successful cider making, both in the factory and at home, depends on the raw material—the apple. Apples are made up of two parts basically—the juice and the solid. If *all* the solubles were extracted from the apple only 4% of the hard matter would be left—but this is a difficult process and usually only 75% of the juice can be extracted at a first pressing, a further 10% at a second. With unripe apples the proportion of juice is naturally less. It is therefore essential to use ripe apples to make the whole process economical.

The acidity of the juice is principally due to malic acid and the quantity depends on the type of apple. There are about five hundred varieties of apples in England alone, half of which would be useless in the making of cider. The table variety of apple contains far more acids than the cider variety. Rough flavoured apples are generally believed to be best for cider making and in the West country there are large numbers of unnamed apples ideal for this, but the most popular are the Cherry Norman, Kingston Black, Red Streak and Hagloe Crab. Cider used to be made from one variety at a time only, but now various types are mixed to make different blends. Cider apples are improved by being weathered, and in some regions, though this is looked down on in others, they are shaken from the tree and put in piles on the grass and left to be affected by the wind and the sun till the skins turn yellow and wrinkle.

Temperatures are also important in cider making. The colder the better, the longer the delay the better. The best time for ripening of apples is not the best time for making cider.

Old English methods for the making of cider retained the pips as it was considered that this gave a better flavour but experts now believe that this is detrimental.

Cider making at home is no more complicated than the making of other country beverages, but the apples should be crushed before they are pressed so that the juice can run free of the pulp. When no mechanical crusher is available this can be done by using a wooden block in a wooden tub lined, if possible, with stainless steel nails to accelerate the breaking up of the fruit.

The apples should be pounded into a coarse mash and set aside for twenty-four hours at the end of which time the juice should run freely. If a wine press is used the pulp should be placed in a coarse linen bag so that unwanted matter does not get mixed up with the juice.

Squeezing with strong fingers is just as good, or using an old-fashioned clothes mangle has equal effect, but the mangle should have wooden rollers, not rubber, which would contaminate the taste.

The juice should be put in a stone, wooden or glass vessel, filled to at least nine-tenths of its capacity, covered over and left to ferment. It should be kept in a warm place.

Depending on the store and the ripeness of the fruit, fermentation will start within a week, in some ideal cases it will not start within twenty-four hours.

Cider is best fermented in open vessels for the fermentation throws up a crust of lees—such fermentation can last from between four days and a fortnight.

There is a subtle difference between cider and apple wine, the latter being much gentler to the palate and less stark to taste. A very simple recipe for making it with windfalls dates back to the early 18th century:-

Wash the apples, do not peel or remove the core, but cut up in small chunks. Place the pieces in an earthenware vessel and cover them with cooled boiled water. Set aside for twelve days. Strain the juice from the resulting pulp and add two pounds of granulated sugar to every gallon of liquid. Stir well until all the sugar is dissolved. Cover and leave for four days. A scum will form on top of the liquid. Remove this and pour the liquid in bottles. Leave a few days before corking.

MEAD

To many people the idea of drinking mead seems rather comic, like covering oneself with woad or clubbing miniskirted girls in lieu of telling them you think them attractive.

Mead is not old-fashioned, it is antique. It is a forgotten drink, a relic of the past, something one heard about at school along with Boadicea and King Arthur and occasionally brought to mind when dreary old Druids prance around Stonehenge on midsummer nights.

Mead, however, will come into its own again. A prediction. For mead is not only an all round versatile drink capable of replacing sherry on social occasions, wine during meals and liqueur after, it is reputed to promote fertility.

The fertility promotion label is so old that it cannot be

discounted, for mead is solely responsible for that very enjoyable and venerated custom the "Honeymoon".

Honeymoons were started by Norsemen who celebrated a wedding not for one day, but for a whole lunar month. Mead kept the bride and bridegroom going during the whole of the long feast, and it kept everyone else going as well. Honey, in the form of drink, was consumed for as long as the moon lasted—hence—Honey Moon.

Mead, in fact, is probably the oldest alcoholic drink on record. It dates back to long before the Roman conquest and was compared by early poets to nectar, the drink of the Greek Gods, for "Nothing could be purer or more wonderful than honey flavoured with honeysuckle, clover, heather, and flowers from the meadow in spring."

Honey was a very important food among the Northern races of Europe, the Scandinavians, Icelanders, Irish Picts, the Scots and Welsh, so much so that the Romans when invading Britain and building their great walls followed a scorched earth policy by burning up fields of heather in order to starve the natives who depended on it for their supply of honey.

The original Druids drank mead in Ireland and Wales and were known by historians as "milk and honey eaters." A historian in 1604 wrote of them and of mead:-

"The Druids and old British bards were wont to carouse thereof, before they entered into speculations. But this drink carries a kind of state with it, for it must always be attended by a brown toast, nor will it admit of but one good draught, and that in the morning; if more, it will keep a humming in the head, and so speak much of the house it comes from, I mean, the hive."

It was the favourite drink of the Saxons who gulped it down from tumblers that had to be emptied quickly for they were like very large spoons and could not stand upright. In the Dark Ages mead was regarded as a status symbol. One, named Hrothgar, built a Mead Hall as an addition to his palace to out-Jones all his neighbours. Mead was also drunk as a toast to victory and sipped, rather morbidly, out of the scooped out skulls of enemies.

The staple drink at King Arthur's court was mead, according to legend and in the Welsh saga 'Mabinogion' it is again mentioned. In the sixth century Taliesin, a respected bard wrote, in his SONG OF TALIESIN:-

> From the mead-horn—the pure shining liquor,
> Which the bees provide but do not enjoy.
> Mead distilled I praise—its eulogy is everywhere,
> Precious to the creature the earth maintains.
> God made it for man, for his happiness;
> The fierce and the humble both enjoy it.

Thomas a Beckett as Archbishop of Canterbury forbade his monks and priests to "peg" mead. Pegging was the custom of passing round a huge tankard which had peg markings down the sides showing the amount each person had drunk. This ruling did not stop the monks, however, who managed to convince themselves that it was necessary as a refreshment on their long pilgrimages to see the Archbishop. It was sometimes called Braggon and was mentioned as such by Bunyan in Pilgrim's Progress.

Whistling for mead was an Elizabethan custom. Special tankards were made of red glass with gold or silver whistles attached to the brim. Whenever the tankard was emptied the owner blew his whistle and the host saw to it that it was re-filled. Queen Elizabeth I herself was a mead drinker and had a Royal tankard made with a special whistle built into the bottom. When the tankard was empty it whistled of its own accord, a sort of murmuring whisper sounding like "meed."

Sir Walter Raleigh had an ostrich egg cup for his mead

drinking. It was mounted in silver, gilded and had the words "Iy Ye want more Ye must wissel for it" engraved on it.

Mead was a common enough drink in the English home until household brewing started to decline, but in the 17th century a recipe for 'Meath' read as follows:-

"Take four quarts of water, and one of honey. Over night stir in one way with your arm for two hours, and after let it stand covered till the morning. Then boyle it till the scum bee taken away, and then put into it a bagg of spice: half Nutmeg, a few cloves, and a little Mace; a little after put into it a sprig or two of Pellitory of the wall and as much Gramoney. Let the Meath boyle till the fifth part bee boyled away; which you must know by a stick with notches in it, then strain it, and let it coole, well covered till next morning. Then turn it and leave the bagg of spice in the Meath till you bottle it, you may put a little Lead in the bag to make it sink. It is sometimes six months, or sometimes a whole year before it bee quite clear, and fitt to be bottled, for you must not bottle it till it be clear."

Another recipe was known as King Charles I Mead:-

"Take 24 quarts of Spring Water, 12 pounds of honey of clover. Stir it well together and stir againe one way only, lett it stand in the kettle you will boyle it in, till the honey is all melted. The King Charles liketh it veery thick, then beat the white of 50 eggs with the shells, beat them very well, then stir them well into your honey and water. Hang the kettle over a clear fire, for Smoke it must not touch, and be shore not to touch it till it boyles. Then Skim it clean, and when it boyled one houre strain it. When it is colld put three Spoonfuls of New Yeast to it, let it stand two days before you tunn it, open. When it have done working slice in Lemmone peel and all 12 cloves, two large blades of Mace, a little Ginger, and bag a Nutmeg and hang it in the Barrill. In six weeks bottle it. It was at that age that the King took it for The Tired Cold and quiet to anxiety he did have after the Wet of Travailles—Here in this House he did take it, as it were In His Grace's Own Home."

In the reign of George III this recipe was made for the Prince of Wales (Later George IV)

"Take of clover honey, from the western counties, pure heather from Spain and heather honey from Scotland, in equal parts. Then take half the quantity in rose and clover honey from England, or Greece (if it be obtainable), and half in orange blossom honey from Italy or Spain. Take the amount required of strong ale, or barley wine and stir the honey into it. Stir it once from 12 to 14 hours continuously, changing your man as soon as his beat becomes slack or tired. Young and strong men do it best. Let it stand for 12 hours then bring it to the boil and skim it well. After an hour take it off and strain it. When it is almost cold put in the white of eggs whipped and a bag containing green pine cones, and honey combs, pieces of ginger, fresh Damask roses, a lime or lemon, and some dried orange blossoms. Stir for two hours the other way, leave for four days, then add your piece of toast with yeast and work it for ten days. Put it in a cask and rack it after 6 weeks into another cask. Rack it 3 times at intervals of 6 weeks until it is ready to bottle. Mature it for one year at least."

Throughout the ages of Western civilization there have been four staple drinks—wine, beer, cider and mead. Of these mead has been the only one to suffer a total eclipse, yet it is the easiest of the four to manufacture.

It differs from other drinks in that its base is not the direct product of a plant but of an insect, the nectar having been gathered by the bee and turned to honey.

Each kind of honey makes a different kind of mead. Honey that is light in colour—clover honey—makes a most beautifully clear, amber mead. Dark honey makes a dark thick Mead. Honey varies greatly in quality depending on the plants of the region, the weather, the apiarist even, and the time of year when the honey is taken from the hive. All this affects the making of mead.

Mead has vintage years, like wine, and premier crus also. The most popular mead in the past was made from virgin honey, the first to be taken from the hive in the Spring, extracted from the combs by pricking the cells lightly and letting the honey drain out without pressure. Spring flowers give the finest scent and taste to the nectar, heather, balm, lime, and gorse but mead made from cowslip honey was a great favourite.

In the Middle Ages when spices were imported from the East a more elaborate mead was made. A spiced mead, laced with various condiments or fortified with brandy and other liquors that came from France. This mead was known as Metheglin, a derivation of the Welsh word for medecine—Medclyglyn. Spiced mead was believed to be a remedy for almost any disease.

Another drink made with honey was Hippocras, known also as a Piment. This type of drink was made with wine, honey and spices and drunk hot. Ginger, cloves, roasted lemon and orange peel were included in some recipes.

The Germans used to mix honey with beer, hardy highlanders honey with whisky which, naturally enough, they drank for breakfast. Vermouth today, is the only descendant of such recipes originally being made with wine and honey—Wein Meth.

CURRANT WINES

"We must buy currants for our wine" wrote Jane Austen to her sister Cassandra in June 1811. It was not the first time she had written about home-made wines or currants, for most ladies in the 19th century spent a good deal of time thinking wine-making if in the end they never quite got down to it. In her day it was considered a social necessity to offer wine, as indeed it still is to-day, though the usual offer is sherry, gin or whisky. None but the most destitute of families were without a wholesome and agreeable drink on the table, and as many were unable to afford an imported wine they made their own. Currant wine was most popular.

Currants are natives of this country and they grow practically everywhere, mainly in woods and forests of the north. Cultivated varieties are hardy and abundant but picking them is a slow and tedious business which puts up the cost of commercial products made from them.

Black currants which are rich in flavour do not make a good wine, in fact in the 19th century it was regarded as having "a stinking and somewhat loathing flavour". Though this is a bit hard on the black currant, there is no doubt that it is very inferior to its colleagues the red and the white. Hot black currant wine, drunk on a cold winter's night, however is both refreshing and pleasantly health-giving.

Whereas the black currant is sweet, the fruit of the red currant has an acid flavour. It makes a tasty dessert and is highly esteemed for the making of tarts and jams, but above all for wine. Red currant wine made in June will be just right for Christmas, but if kept till the following year will be even better.

A 17th century herbalist wrote of the red currant that it was "recommended to extinguish or mitigate fevers, repress choler, temper over-hot blood and to resist putrefaction."

In 1834 this recipe for red currant wine making was published for the benefit of housewives:-

"Choose the ripest red currants, put them into crocks and expose them to mellow. Then put them into a closed vessel and put it into a slow oven or kiln, or directly upon the fire in a vessel of water, and heat it slowly to a temperature of 145 degrees Fahrenheit, at which heat keep it for half an hour. Raise the heat then to 170 degrees and, finally, very gradually to 200 degrees, or just below boiling-point. During this coction the juice of the fruit will be mollified in its pellicle, or skin, and will flow quite clear, whereas had it been bruised or pressed the juice would have been cloudy and its viscosity would have prevented it from clarifying. This virgin must is so sweet that it is not necessary to add sugar or some other sweet, except to raise the specific gravity, for without gravity there is no alcohol and neither alcohol nor flavour will please.

Instead of using sugar we may use honey or the juice of dried raisins, for these latter contain an excess of 'saccharum' which is especially required for the fabrication of sweet wines. To extract this saccharum, the raisins must be macerated in a cask or small vessel, with some white wine, and be allowed to stand for several months. When the wine is drawn off, and the raisins pressed, an excellent sacharrine solution is procured which will increase the gravity of any wine to which it is added. The must also gains particular flavour and is given an aroma of the most agreeable kind. The sweets, of whatever kind employed, are best introduced after

55

the currant juice has flowed clear and before the temperature falls below 70 degrees, for in between that and 65 degrees, the must should be put into the tun or cask, awaiting spontaneous fermentation."

The recipe for white currant wine making dating from the same period is virtually the same. White currants, however are sweeter than red currants.

ELDERBERRY WINE

As far as many post-war Londoners are concerned elderberry wine first made its appearance on the scene when laced with arsenic by two old ladies in the play ARSENIC AND OLD LACE. From then on the drink was frowned on as somewhat dubious and lost what little popularity it had.

It is, however, like all other fruit wines, now coming back into its own.

Elderberries have figured in the history of British wine making for as long as beer has. It was made by the Druids, it was drunk throughout the Middle Ages and in Jacobean times everyone who was anyone was drinking Elder Posset, a concoction invented by homecoming crusaders loaded with strange Eastern herbs and roots. Their recipe ran as follows :-

"To a hogshead of strong ale take a heap'd vessel of elderberries and a half pound of juniper berries beaten; put in all the berries when you put in the hops and let them boil together till the berries break in pieces; then work it up as you do ale. When it has done working add to it half a pound of ginger, half an ounce of cloves, as much mace, an ounce of nutmegs, and as much cinnamon grossly beaten, half a pound of citron, as much eringo root, and likewise candied orange peel. Let the sweetmeats be cut in pieces very thin, and put with the spice into a bag, and hang it in the vessel when you stop it up, and drink it with lumps of double-refined sugar in the glass."

In the 17th century also a certain Lady Fenetta Hyde wrote the following in her home-recipe book:-

"Take twenty pounds of Malaga raisins picked, rubbed and chopped, but not washed, to five gallons of water. Let them stand ten days then strain the liquor through a hair sieve; have in readiness five pounds of the juice of elderberries, being infused in a mug. Put into a kettle of water as you do for syrup and when the juice is cold, put it in a vessel and let it stand in a warm place for six weeks with a yeast toste, see that it be covered during the working. Bottle it and keep in a cool cellar for at least one year. You must be careful that the berries bees full ripe, but not inclining to the rotten.
Note: The water must boil one hour and be put boiling hot to the raisins and stirred well once a day all of ten days. Keep it close covered."

In the 18th century the making of elderberry wine was a fairly big business, so much so that orchards of elder were grown in Kent and the fruit was sent to the London markets where it was bought by the bushel for the making of wine and syrups. It was also bought by cloth manufacturers who used the berries for making dyes and by herbalists who made medicine. The elderberry is an astringent and a cathartic.

A glass of hot mulled elderberry wine taken before going to bed is one of the better ways of getting rid of colds and of soothing any bronchial troubles. In the past it was a standard drink sold in pubs and regarded as the most wholesome drink, its consumption seeming to promote good health.

An 18th century recipe runs as follows:-

"In the proportions of two gallons of water to one of Berries, which must be clean picked from the Stalks and boiled half an hour; then strained through a hair sieve. Measure your liquor and to every gallon, put three pounds of sugar, boil it again till the sugar is quite dissolved, and skim it well. Add to 12 gallons of the wine two ounces of cloves and one ounce of Jamaica Pepper and likewise a little ginger tied up in a linen and put in after it is clear of scum, and boil up in the wine. Put the wine in a large tub to cool, and when it is near cold put a bit of bread dipped in New Yeast into it, to work it, let it stand a week and then tunn it again. Take off the Head clean before you put it into the Cask, which should be covered slightly till it has quite done working —near a month—when some brandy, about half a pint of brandy to a gallon of wine, should be put in and stopped close. If it does not ferment in a day or two, toast a fresh piece of bread and dip it in Yeast, and warm a little of the wine and put it into a basin covered over for 12 hours then put that to the rest and stir it about. If you make 12 gallons of liquor, the quantity of berries before mentioned will allow of 2 gallons more water."

The elder grows anywhere. In the middle of cities, on bomb sites, in gardens, parks and everywhere in the country. It is a fragrant flowering shrub but not the type which is cultivated for its beauty, it is an untidy plant and more of a shrub "happening."

In the 17th century an eccentric Dutch physician spent a good deal of his time promoting the elder, and let it be known widely that he respected it so much that he thought it proper to take his hat off every time he passed an elder. As he lived in Holland this was perhaps acceptable, but had he lived in England he would not have found it worth while wearing a hat at all.

The abundant clusters of fruit and flowers the elder produces are easily picked because the tree is short and often bears its harvest low down. There are no thorns to scratch, and the smell of the tree makes the picking pleasant.

Elderberry was used to give many wines a better colour, especially vin rose as the hue of this particular wine was often difficult to attain, the pigment in grape skin varying from year to year. Stringent laws had to be imposed against its use as a colouring agent and it is now used in moderation if at all.

In England an even worse fraud involved the innocent berry. In the 19th century a reputable wine merchant, in a large University town, sold elderberry wine under various labels and made a handsome profit. Imitations of port, claret and burgundy wines made from elderberry were sold in vast quantities to dons and undergraduates who eulogised its vintages knowledgeably. A number of people in the business suspected the outrage because they knew how little real wine was being imported and could see the outstanding amount being sold, but there was no proof, and no certainty. Eventually this happy merchant retired a rich man and only on his deathbed did he tell his son the truth. Most of the famous wines he had sold had been made with elderberry, then adapted, flavoured and coloured with brown sugar and vinegar to suit the bottle and label.

Though it is still likely to be denied to-day there are some founders' ports in colleges and universities throughout the country which are not in fact port at all—but elderberry wine.

Many people regard elderberry wine as a winter drink,

and in parts of the country farmers families' still mull it when the snow keeps them away from the fields and their work. A present day recipe for mulled elderberry wine runs as follows:-

"Make a large earthenware jug hot, pour into it a bottle of Merrydown Elderberry Wine and warm it by the stove. Rub the skin of a lemon with a few lumps of sugar, and when they have got the taste of lemon, drop them into the wine. Squeeze the juice of the lemon in and a little grated nutmeg. When all is well mixed pour in a quart of boiling water, stir, then add a glass of brandy."

GOOSEBERRY WINE

The gooseberry has an amusing enough name, it is a strange enough looking fruit but it also has a reputation, for of all the fruits from which wines can be made it is the gooseberry that has been most successful in imitating the king of all wines-Champagne.

In France, in the 18th century, so much gooseberry wine was sold as a substitute for champagne that it gradually lost its reputation as a good wine in itself. It became a fraudulent wine and to offer it as champagne was very nearly an insult to the guest, yet as a fruit wine it was in fact superb. Obviously it could never have reached a point when dishonest publicans served it as champagne if it had not been.

A secondary fermentation can start when the gooseberry shrub flowers and if caught in this state a sparkling wine results. It should be made in June when the gooseberries are well grown but still green and acid, and the cask should be put aside till the following April when the wine should be bottled off. The bottles should be laid down for six months, after which it will sparkle. Not all gooseberry wines need of course sparkle. Bottled at other times of the year the gooseberry will make a very pleasant still wine. A recipe for such a still wine dates some time back:-

GOOSYBERRI WINE

"Take a peck of verry ripe Goosberries, but not bursted, break them in a stone mortar, and strain out the juice through a verry thinne cloth, wringing very hard, let the juice stand two or three days in an Earthen potte, stire it about once a day, then take two pounds of loaf sugar, and the rest put into a gallon of water and boyle it about half an houre, then out it a cooling till it be quite colde. Then run the Goosyberri liquid through a jelly bag, as along as it will runne clear, and to every pint of liquor made with the sugar and water, add a pint of Rennish wine. And soe bottle up with a lump of sugar. It being well worked will bee fitte to drink in a fortnight or thereabouts."

ORANGE WINE

A Very Simple and Easy Way to Make Very Superior Orange Wine—according to Mrs Beeton:-

"Ingredients: 90 Seville Oranges, 32 lbs Sugar. Water. Mode: Break up the sugar into small pieces and put it into a dry, sweet nine-gallon cask, placed in a cellar or other store-house where it is intended to be kept. Have ready close to the cask two large pans or keelers (flat bottomed wooden vessels) into one of which put the peel of the fruit pared quite thin, and into the other the pulp after the juice has been squeezed from it. Strain the juice through a piece of double muslin and put it in the cask with double sugar. Then pour about one and a half gallons of cold spring water on to both peel and the pulp; let it stand for twenty-four hours, and then strain it into the cask; add more water to the peels and pulp when this is done and repeat the same process every day for a week; in a week the cask should be about full.

"Be careful to apportion the quantity as near as possible to the seven days, and to stir the contents of the cask every day. On the third day after the cask is full —that is, the tenth day after the commencement of making—the cask may be securely bunged down.

"This is a very simple and easy method and the wine made according to it will be pronounced excellent. There is no troublesome boiling and all the fermentation takes place in the cask. When the above directions are attended to the wine cannot fail to be good. It should be bottled in eight or nine months and will be fit for use in a twelvemonth after the time of making.

Time: Ten days to make it.

Sufficient for nine gallons.

Seasonable. Make it in March and bottle it the following January."

The above is, probably, as simple as Mrs Beeton is determined it should be.

The results will depend on you, and the drink may or may not be appreciated by your guests. In the past orange wine was drunk by sherry drinkers as a substitute, the taste and tang being similar. It was drunk from small glasses—sherry glasses—before meals as an appetiser.

GRAIN, HERB, TREE AND VEGETABLE WINES

Whisky and beer result from the fermented grains of barley. Wheat does not malt so well so it is less commonly used. Manioc, maize, millet and rice all make drinks, but only in the countries where they are grown in quantity.

Manioc is the root of the tapioca plant—this is made into a beer in Africa and South America.

A mixture of maize and molasses was made by the North American Indians and was so hot that it became famous as 'Fire Water'. It was also called Hoochinoo and eventually was reduced to the present day American-loved "Hooch."

Millet can only be purchased in England to-day as bird-seed, but it can be made into a powerful enough drink. Wine made from rice is probably the oldest wine ever made and is much preferred in the far East to grape wine.

In a book written by Samuel Moreland—HISTORY OF INEBRIATING LIQUORS, the following description is given on how to make rice wine.

"The grain is steeped for twenty to thirty days in cold water, and then gently boiled. When it is soft and pulpy and completely dissolved by the heat it is allowed a considerable time to ferment in vats, made especially for that purpose, of glazed earthenware. The yeast employed is of wheat, in which several wholesome ingredients are added during the process of fermentation; these consist of such fruits and flowers as impart an agreeable flavour and pleasing colour. At the end of several days when the motion and agitation occasioned by the fermenting process has subsided, and when the liquor has thrown up all the scum and dross, it is drawn off into glazed vessels, where, by a second species of fermentation, it clears itself and develops, by the taste and smell, its good or bad qualities. When sufficiently fined it is put into small jars and sold throughout the Empire. This wine is usually so strong that it will keep for many years—some say ages. The lees are distilled into an agreeable sort of hot spirit called 'choo,' 'Samt-Choo' or burnt wine."

If this rice wine sounds a little too hot, too spirited, a far cry from the Far East can bring one back to the English country garden and a wine which grows, to any horticulturalist's intense displeasure, in great abundance. Nettle wine.

The Romans used nettles to get their athletes going. Under the pretence that by stinging themselves they got rid of any possible cramp or arthritis, they rubbed nettles over their legs, arms and other limbs in order to keep fit. They believed so much in this that they brought the nettle to our shores along with the grape. Who first thought of making wine out of the wretched plant is not recorded, but the following is a recipe for anyone who wishes to indulge:

"Gather two gallon containers full of young spring nettle shoots, use only the tops, wash them and put them into a saucepan with two gallons of water, a race of ginger, four pounds of malt, two ounces of hops and, if liked, four ounces of sarsaparilla. Bring all to the boil and keep it so for a quarter of an hour, then strain it onto a pound of sugar. When this has dissolved and the liquor is at a temperature of 45 degrees Fahrenheit, beat some yeast to a froth in a little of the liquor and add it to the beer. Put all into beer bottles and screw down the corks. It will be ready for drinking in twelve hours."

Parsley wine is still found being made in remote districts where the inhabitants drink it for their health and praise it highly as an antidote to the scourge of rheumatism. To have any effect at all, however, it must be drunk regularly and this, if you find it tastes a little like medicine, can become a bore rather than a pleasure.

To make parsley wine take a pound of parsley to every

gallon of water. Put the leaves in a container and pour the boiling water on them. Infuse for twenty-four hours. In a pan put four pounds of sugar or honey, the juice and rind of two oranges and two lemons. Strain the infusion onto these and stir until the sugar has dissolved, then add an ounce of yeast and leave to stand for four days in a warm place. When the fermentation has declined, bottle the wine. It can be drunk immediately but will improve with age.

Another medicinal herb wine is that made with balm leaves. Known sometimes as balsam it used to be given by country people to those suffering from hysteria or nervous diseases. One famous herbalist wrote that "It causeth the mind to become merry and reviveth the faint heart. It driveth away all troublesome cares and thought out of the mind, arising from melancholy or black choler."

Take two quarts of balm leaves, to make it, and put them in a crock. Boil a gallon of water, add two pounds of sugar, the juice and rind of a lemon and the beaten white of an egg. Skin well and strain onto the leaves and stir till it is cool. Float a piece of yeasted toast on the liquid and leave to ferment for two or three days. Strain through a muslin cloth into a cask filling it to the top. When all the working has stopped, seal it well and leave for three months.

Balm wine, like wormwood or camomile, is bitter to the taste and would be enjoyed by those who now revel in the sophisticated delights of campari.

For those hell bent on tasting every possible kind of wine, a little walk in any garden should provide ample possibilities. Palm wine, made from the palm tree, must unfortunately be the joy only of those who live in Torquay, Penzance, the South of France or Equatorial regions, but for others the method by which the walnut, the sycamore, and the birch are tapped should be carefully noted.

Tree tapping requires skill and experience to make sure that the tree itself is not permanently injured. A tube made from a branch of the elder from which the soft pith has been removed should be used, stuck into the side of the tree and the sap allowed to run out. Or rather ooze out. It is the depth to which the tube is sunk that matters.

When a sufficient quantity of sap has been collected then the actual operation of ¦making tree wine can begin. In 1795 a Miss Elizabeth Raffald wrote out these two invaluable recipes. For sycamore wine﹕

"Take two gallons of sap of a sycamore tree, boil it half an hour, then add to it four or five pounds of fine powdered sugar. Beat the whites of three eggs to a froth and mix them with the liquor, but if it·is too hot it will poach the eggs. Scum it very well and beat it for half an hour, then strain it through a hair sieve and let it stand till the next day. Pour it clean from the sediment, put in a quarter of a pint of good yeast to every twelve gallons, cover it up closely with blankets till it is white over, then put it in a barrel till it is done working. Close the bung and let the barrel stand for three months before bottling; the fifth part of the sugar should be loaf and if you like raisins they are a great addition to the wine."

For oak and walnut wine she managed to avoid using the sap and only the leaves, which is one way of getting rid of them in the Autumn if the damp air or rain forbids a bonfire.

"To every gallon of water put three and a half pounds of honey and boil together for three-quarters of an hour. To each gallon of liquor obtained put two dozen oak/walnut leaves and pour the liquor boiling hot upon

66

them. Let them stand all night and then take out the leaves and put in a spoonful of yeast. Let it work for two or three days and then make up the quantity to fill the cask. Let it stand for three months, then bottle."

The Emperor Tiberius liked parsnip wine. He was one of the few people of note who said so and despite this it has never actually acquired a reputation of being a wine served on important occasions. Parsnip wine has remained, despite its very important beginnings, a humble, unrecognized country wine. One Nicholas Culpepper in the ENGLISYH PHYSICIAN AND COMPLETE HERBAL wrote in 1653 the following about it, however:

"The garden Parsnip is under Venus; it nourisheth much, and is very good and wholesome, but a little windy, whereby it is thought to procure bodily lust—the wild being better than the garden show Dame Nature to be the best physician."

To make parsnip wine you should apparently dig them up in the autumn and lay them out to be well frosted as this will increase the sugar content. When they are ready they should be taken indoors, scrubbed well and cut into small pieces. They should be weighed and a gallon of water used to every four or five pounds of parsnips.

To every gallon add the thinly peeled rind of two lemons and one orange. Heat but do not cover when the liquor starts boiling as the aroma of the parsnip is rather strong. Strain the liquid onto three pounds of sugar or honey and stir until all is well blended together. When the liquor is cool, float on a piece of ale-yeasted toast.

Cover the vessel for three days, skimming off the excess of yeast that forms on the surface, then strain again into a cask, keeping it well filled with some portion of the liquor set aside for this purpose. Bottle off after six months and, to make the wine more powerful, drive in the corks firmly.

For those who fear spiders there is a wine too. Celery wine. Though drinking it alone does not frighten them away, the imbibing of a bottle or two will prevent the bite of venomous spiders from harming you— or so our forefathers believed.

Celery wine should be made with the white parts of the stems and roots only, not the leaves.

To each pound of white celery put one quart of water, boil until the vegetable is soft and limp, but remove from the fire before the fibres begin to break up or the liquor clouded. Strain it onto three pounds of brown sugar for each gallon, and put into a cask. Add yeast and, when the excess fermentation has subsided, fill up the cask, bung down and keep in store before drinking.

Mangold and carrot wines are made in a similar way to parsnip wine but turnip wine has a different recipe. This one dates from the 18th century:

"Pare and slice what quantity of turnips you like and put them into a cider press. Squeeze out what juice you can. To every gallon use three pounds of lump sugar, put both into a vessel large enough to hold them and add to every gallon half a pint of brandy. Lay something over the bung for a week, and, when it is worked, bung it down close. Let stand for three months and then draw it off into another vessel. Fine it and bottle."

No book on English wines could be thought complete without a recipe for mangold-wurzel wine. The author has not tried this presumably palatable delight but strongly advises the addict to "any" wine to try it at least once.

A gallon container full of mangold wurzels should be picked, the vegetables cleaned, washed and the roots removed.

They should be cut up and put to boil in a gallon of water.

They should be strained.

3 lbs. of sugar should be added to the liquid and stirred till dissolved.

$\frac{1}{2}$ oz. of hops should be added and when the liquid is cooler 1 oz. of yeast.

The wine should be left to ferment for three weeks, then strained and bottled.

WINES FOR THE FLOWER CHILDREN

Towards the end of 1967, when the flower children were at their most colourful, it struck me as strange that they did not extend their generosity of giving away flowers to those who did not like them. A glass of flower wine would not only have cooled the tempers of the drab, but also rendered them slightly happy. And the happiness was surely what the children wished to promote. Perhaps, now that the first generation have gone forth and multiplied, they will pass on some of the following recipes to their grand flower children, for surely the smelling of scents and the appreciation of beauty can only be followed by the swallowing of the flower.

There is no limit to the wines which can be made with flowers, it is only a matter of going out into the country and picking. Roses, dandelion, marigolds, primroses, cowslip, elder, coltsfoot, all can be turned into pleasant tasting liquids without too much trouble, and surely to toast the health of a flower cult to the music of the sitar would, as a total flower experience, be more rewarding with a glass of agrimony wine in hand than a mug of coke.

The first thing to do is pick the roses and remove the petals. These should be packed into a quart jar so as to measure their quantity. Having a quart of rose petals, a quart of boiling water should be poured onto them. The petals should be pressed well down with a wooden spoon. When the water is impregnated with the perfume, it should be strained through muslin all the time pressing the petals well so as to extract their juices. Another quart of boiling water should be poured on them and they should be pressed again and the water filtered again.

To the two quarts of rose water thus obtained, two pounds of the finest sugar should be added and the whole boiled for twenty minutes. The scum should be removed continually as it forms. When the water has cooled, yeast should be added and the wine covered over till working has ceased. The wine should then be bottled. The longer it is kept the greater the perfume.

In 1808 a recipe for rose petal wine appeared in the Town and Country Housekeepers' Guide. It was as follows:

"Put into a glazed earthenware vessel three gallons of cold drawn rose water. Put in a sufficient number of rose petals and cover closely. Set all for an hour in a kettle or copper pan of hot water, to extract the whole strength and flavour of the roses. When cold, press the rose petals hard into the liquor and steep fresh ones in it; repeat this till the water has the full strength of the roses. To each gallon of liquor put three pounds of loaf sugar and stir well that it may melt and disperse in every part. Then put into a cask to ferment and throw into it a piece of bread toasted hard and covered with yeast. Let it stand a month. If you add wine or spices it will be a great improvement. By the same mode of infusion, wines may be made from any other flowers that have an odoriferous scent and grateful flavour."

The easiest flower to pick is the dandelion, even the London flower children can find these in the Parks. The dandelion not only allows itself to be made into a wine but it is apparently beneficial to health. Medical history has noted that "It is very effectual for the jaundice and hypochondriacal passions—and whoso is drawing towards consumption, or to an evil disposition of the body. It is good to drink against pestilence fever." To-day it is still recognized as having the virtues of being a blood purifier and diuretic.

The dandelion should be picked on a dry summer's day. The thin yellow petals plucked from the green calyxes and placed in a gallon jar. When the jar is filled they should be removed to a larger container and a gallon of boiling water poured over them. This infusion should last for three days and the mixture stirred regularly each morning. The whole should then be boiled for half an hour with rinds of oranges and lemon, a rootstock of ginger and three pounds of sugar, honey or malt. It should then be left to cool, then a little yeast, on a piece of toast, floated on the top.

The container should be well covered and the whole left till the first fermentation has subsided. It should then be strained, and set aside again well covered before bottling it. The whole operation should take about a month, and the wine is drinkable after about six months.

If the wine is placed in a cask it can be fed with raisins and sugar candy. It has been known for people in the country to have a cask of dandelion wine for over twenty years which they keep on feeding. The older and more fed the wine the stronger it becomes.

The marigold was a favourite wine flower with Elizabethans who not only drank it but used the flower itself in salads. It is supposed to have medicinal properties, a

71

remedy against heart weaknesses, cancer and other ills. The Elizabethans used to dry the petals or candy them, store them in wooden casks or ground them into a powder as well as brew them.

The marigold should be picked on a fine summer's day, at mid-day when they are fully opened. The petals stripped from the calyxes and only the golden petals used. To every "peck" of petals should be added a pound of raisins. This should be boiled in two and half gallons of water to which is added six pounds of sugar or honey. When these ingredients are well stirred and blended a white of an egg should be added.

The following day the mixture should be stirred continually for twenty minutes, and the day following that it should be strained into a cask containing the juice and rind of two oranges and two ounces of sugar candy.

A pint of must should then be drawn from it, warmed and two tablespoonsfulls of yeast added. This fermentation starter should then be added to the cask and the whole covered with a thick cloth.

When the fermentation has ceased a pint of good brandy should be poured in and half an ounce of isinglass dissolved in warm water. The cask should be stopped up and left for nine months before the wine is bottled.

Primroses are one of the prettiest flowers to pick, but do not in fact make quite as good a wine as others.

Six quarts of primroses should be mixed with two quarts of cowslip in a crock. Three gallons of water, eight pounds of loaf sugar, half an ounce of powdered ginger and a few cloves should be boiled and poured over them.

The whole should then be stirred and a pound and a half of stoned raisins and the juice of three lemons added. The vessel should be covered and left for three days.

Take a little of the infusion, warm it, beat into a teaspoonful of yeast and add to the liquor. When fermentation has ceased pour in half a pint of brandy and a little isinglass dissolved in water. The container should then be sealed and stored away for a year. After a year the wine should be bottled but not drunk for at least another six months.

In view of the time it takes to make this wine and its not fantastic taste it might be better to concentrate on cowslip, which is far more rewarding.

Cowslip wine is narcotic. A glass of it at night is more soporific than any other night-cap offered on the television screen. It does not only induce sleep, rather than unconsciousness, but it forms no injurious habits and can be given up when sleep comes naturally again. Cowslip wine was so popular at one time that, apart from Alexander Pope writing about it—"For want of rest, Lettuce and Cowslip; probatum est"—it was made commercially at Worcester where the flowers grew in great abundance.

Only the yellow corolla of the blossom is used as any other part is too bitter. Each flower contains a fair proportion of honey but not enough to do without more honey or sugar. To get the best results cowslip should be kept at least two years, though a year makes a quite passable wine.

Two pounds of sugar should be boiled in a gallon of water for an hour. An ounce of yeast with one and a half ounces of syrup of lemon should be spread on toast. When the water has cooled down, but is still warm, the yeasted toast should be dropped in.

While this is fermenting two gallons of cowslips, two shredded lemons and a bottle of white wine should be added. After three days the liquid poured into a cask, and after five weeks bottled.

A quicker cowslip wine can be made with purple clover flowers as well.

Six pints of both flowers, well mixed, are needed. They should be covered with a gallon of boiling water, and left standing for four days, but covered. The liquid should then be strained and the juice of three lemons, two oranges, 3 lbs of sugar and an ounce of yeast added.

When fermentation has stopped the wine should be stirred then left to settle for three days. It should then be carefully strained and put into a large glass container and corked. After four months it can be bottled and will be at its best after another nine months.

The elder, which grows anywhere but is especially noted for its love of city suburbs, provides two wines—elderberry, already dealt with, and elderflower wine.

Elderflower water used to be used as a cosmetic and could be found on most fine ladies' dressing tables, elderflower ointment was also in great demand in the 18th century, both as cures for skin ailments.

Elderflower drinks are fragrant, light and agreeable, and were said to clear the blood of impurities. They were sipped genteelly in summer gardens on hot days in the shade of trees—elderflower champagne, a petillant wine, being a favourite, elderflower mead, made with honey, proving more popular for the winter.

To make the wine the flowers should be stripped from the stems and only the corollas employed.

A pint mug of flowers well pressed down should be boiled in a gallon of water till the water is a bright golden colour.

In a crock, separately, three pounds of sugar, half a

pound of raisins and the juice and rind of two lemons should be well mixed. On this the infusion is poured through a strainer, the whole then stirred till all the sugar is melted. Taking a cup full of the liquid, add ½ ounce of ale-yeast, stir and then pour back into the crock when the infusion is cold. Cover and store for twenty-four hours.

The liquid should then be strained and poured into a cask which is sealed lightly till all sounds of fermentation have ceased. It should then be bottled and corked down firmly and stored till required. The longer it remains in bottle the better, but it can be drunk after three or four months.

After the fermentation is over and before bottling, a pint of brandy can be added to every gallon of elder-flower wine.

When people suffered from scrofula they always hoped that one day they would meet a King or Queen who would touch them and then they would be cured. Royalty had that power, they thought. If they didn't think this, they believed that coltsfoot would do the trick. Coltsfoot is of great benefit, they said, to those who suffer from chest complaints and they even smoked it instead of tobacco.

Two quarts of coltsfoot flowers should be used in this recipe and mixed with two pounds of raisins and the juice and peel of two lemons. Over them should be poured a syrup made with two pounds of sugar and one gallon of boiling water. A piece of toast, spread with yeast, should be thrown in, and the whole stored in a crock for four days. After the fermentation has worked the liquid should be strained, then bottled. The wine is drinkable after six months, but if it can be kept longer it is better.

It is not one of the best wines to make, but an amusing diversion from those more often made.

Agrimony, like coltsfoot, is not too good on the nose, or indeed superb on the palate, but it does wonders with the bowels, cleans the liver and counteracts the poison of venomous serpents (which is worth noting for any flower children venturing East). It is a remedy against the quartain ague and the bloody flux and, mixed with grease, can be used as an ointment on ulcers.

A good bunch of agrimony should be boiled in two gallons of water with a little crushed ginger. When the water has a nice colour it should be poured, hot, onto seven pounds of sugar, the rind and juice of six oranges and six lemons and a lump of root ginger. It should be allowed to infuse for six days before being strained into a cask and allowed to ferment. Once covered it should be left six months before drinking.

For admirers of Proust a simple hawthorn wine can be made in the merry month of May.

Put ½ gallon of the May hawthorn blossom in a bowl and pour over it a syrup made with 3 lbs. of sugar and a gallon of boiling water. Allow to cool. When cold put in a pound of wheat, ½ pound of raisins and an ounce of yeast spread on toast. Leave it to ferment for a fortnight stirring well every day. Then bottle.

A stronger hawthorn wine can be made by mixing a gallon of hawthorn flowers with 2 oz. of crumbled lump ginger and one pound of raisins, two finely sliced oranges and one finely sliced lemon. After the mixture has been allowed to stand for two or three hours, a boiling syrup made of 3 lbs. of sugar and 1 gallon of water should be poured over. When the whole has cooled, a piece of yeasted toast should be dropped in. The Hawthorn mixture should then be allowed to ferment for a fortnight before being strained off and bottled.

5

How to be a Wine Snob

HOW TO BE A
WINE SNOB

Before embarking seriously on any form of wine drinking
it seems that you must, according to the various books I
have read on the subject, adopt a definite attitude towards
the way you drink and the way others drink.

There are two schools of thought on this problem. The
first is that there are good wines and bad wines, as there is
good art and bad art. The supposition that "the wine you
like is a good wine" is apparent nonsense and as ridiculous
as "the picture you like is a good picture" or "the music
you like is good music". There are, in fact, only better
wines and worse wines and these can only be distinguished
by those whose taste has been trained by experience and
knowledge, and it is obvious that the more exquisite savours
of wine, as the higher pleasures of art, can only be enjoyed
by those who have given intelligent attention to the matter.
That is the first thought.

The second is simpler. Wine is for drinking. It is not for

worshipping, being one up on the Joneses, nor for proving how frightfully cosmopolitan and sophisticated you are or how intelligent. There is no mystique about it. Like any drink, from soda water to venerable vintage port, there are some conditions in which it tastes better than others, but then the same applies to tea or coffee. What you drink is a personal matter—let no one tell you otherwise.

Thus armed with these two arguments it is up to the wine drinker to decide which team he is going to belong to, and behave in the appropriate manner. Wine drinkers, it must be remembered, are continually watched—by head waiters, sommeliers, other wine drinkers and total amateurs.

To be the perfectionist, whichever side you favour, you must know the rules—either to obey them strictly and thus be in a position to cast a disapproving eye on someone who doesn't—or to break them deliberately and thus cast a disapproving eye on someone who does observe them.

The following are the rules. Practise them and you will be accepted among the best of wine snobs. Break them and you will be accepted among the best anti-wine-snob snobs. If you don't know them you can't win. If you do know them you can't lose.

First remember to serve and drink wines in an order which will produce a crescendo of effect on the human sensory apparatus. Stronger wines should be kept till last because the weaker ones will seem weaker after the strong ones, and as a dinner progresses one's sensibility diminishes. It is heresy to drink port after soup as this kills all wines that follow. Obviously.

The proper wine order at a dinner should be CHABLIS or POUILLY with oysters and fish. A Beaujolais, light BURGUNDY or BORDEAUX with the entree. The Grand Crus, a CHATEAU wine, a VOUGEOT or

CHAMBERTIN with roast or game. A BEAUNE, POMMARD or dry CHAMPAGNE with veal, Sweet CHAMPAGNE or Demi Sec should be taken with the dessert, and before coffee a glass of port—afterwards a COGNAC or ARMAGNAC.

It is impossible to appreciate the savours of these wines unless you are deliberately elegant and extravagant in the manner in which you taste them. The room, table, the company, the shape and quality of the glasses, makes a difference. All these must be chosen to suit the wine. After some experiments you will find which setting suits your Pouilly best, which friends seem to blend correctly with the Chambertin, which glasses give the best nose to your Pommard. This can be an expensive process if you wish to savour several wines and some of your friends blend incorrectly with the wines of your choice. It is best, therefore, to have various rooms full of different friends in order to avoid disappointment.

Temperature is all important—as everyone knows. White wines should be a few degrees colder than the room, and in warm weather full bodied white wines may even be iced.

Red wines should have been given time to "take" the temperature of the room—a matter of two to three hours —and there is no objection about it being one or two degrees above it, but if this is overdone then its finer qualities will disappear and the aroma which it gives off will be so loaded with alcohol that the perfume will become indistinguishable.

The wine glass should be as thin as possible so that the wine is affected by the slightest degree of warmth from the hand. It should be of a bulging shape with its opening smaller than its body so that the bouquet given off may be inhaled as though concentrated through a funnel.

The glass should never be more than half full and the connoisseur should begin the process of drinking by tilting it gently so that he may visually appreciate the beauty of its colour then, with the glass steady, inhale the power of the wine with his nose.

The base of the glass should be held between forefinger and thumb and a rotary movement gradually increasing in speed given to the liquid. A good wine will offer a complete scale of scents, delicate, subtle, powerful, and the expert will thus be able to distinguish accurately from the resulting sensations the year, if not the month, of the vintage, its place of origin and, in some cases, the name of the shipper.

Wine should be drunk as birds drink water, in little sips. It should be rolled attentively round the tongue, for each part of the tongue has its special sensibility, its varying taste buds.

Before swallowing, the lips should be pursed up and a little air drawn in to mingle with the wine, now at the same temperature as the mouth. This action will be rewarded by a new series of sensations.

The wine should not be allowed to stand long in the glass before being sipped, and the true gourmet knows of course that the best time to taste wine is first thing in the morning before anything else has had a chance to soil the palate.

Violent exercises are disastrous to tasting and there should be no noise or conversation to distract or hamper the mental concentration which is necessary if the full beauty of a great wine is to be appreciated.

Each wine should be respected as having a temperament and individuality of its own. Champagne is always respected by most people simply because of its price, but others should be given as much care and attention. It is essential to remember never to put ice in champagne, but around it. Ice is not always perfectly clean and when it melts it can cloud a wine.

Decanting other wines should always be done carefully, if at all. All wines throw a deposit, the deposit in a sound wine indicates an improvement, but is not required for consumption and should be left in the bottle. Its presence in a decanter not only spoils the flavour but the appearance. When decanting very old wines, such as port, it is best to remove the neck of the bottle completely by breaking it off with a special pair of tongs which, when heated, and squeezed round the bottle, snap off the top cleanly.

The vessel into which wines are decanted is important too. A decanter should be chosen to show off the wine's colour and should therefore be of clear glass, never coloured.

Port and sherry are always poured from heavy, broad based or onion shaped decanters. All other wines from finer glass with delicately shaped necks allowing the light to shine through. Extravagance in a decanter is not a sign of good winemanship, the least cut, the least decorated, the plainer the decanter the better. There is nothing more beautiful to the wine snob than light filtering through the simple curve of a fine decanter first thing in the morning.

Glasses are even more important, directly affecting the taste of the wine. Again coloured glass should never be used, even though some Alsatian wines are sometimes served in green glass. It does nothing, in fact, to enhance the pure colour of the wine, and should really be avoided. Wine cannot be drunk with the completest appreciation by anyone who does not understand the part the eye plays in the tasting.

For champagne the best glass is not what is commonly known as a champagne glass—that is the shallow bowl-like glass on a thin stem—but the flute glass, a deep tulip shaped vessel. The ideal claret and burgundy drinking glasses are those with equally proportioned bowls. For the drinking of port, old glasses are suitable, with thick glass. For sherry experts recommend a long thin glass only half filled.

The cleaning of glasses is very important. They should always be polished and shining, but never cleaned with soap suds.

Brandy glasses should not be too small, but large enough to give the bouquet a chance. Fashions dictate the size and shapes of brandy glasses, but generally simple, small balloons are advised. The large, vast balloons are amusing, but are termed buffoon balloons by the snob. Brandy is a pleasant discreet drink, one should not show off when imbibing it.

Fine glass should be washed in water, rinsed, then polished. Decanters should never be washed inside with detergents but cleaned by shaking small shot about in them.

Last, but by no means least, the rules of serving should be learnt by heart:

A good wine should never be served with a salad or any other dish which has been seasoned with vinegar or sugar.

If two of the same wines—but of different vintages—are served at the same sitting, the younger wine of the two should be served first.

A few wine terms to slip knowledgeably into the conversation.

AGE. Meaning the age of the wine. "It has age" sounds pleasant to the snob.
BEESWING. A light, filmy, floating crust in some old ports.
BODY. The quality in a wine which gives it the appearance of vinous strength.
BOUQUET. The odour or perfume of a wine.

BRUT. Champagne in its most natural state. With no added sugar.

CHATEAU BOTTLED. Wines bottled at the Chateau where grown as opposed to wine-merchant bottled.

CORKED. A bad smelling wine. A mouldy wine which has gone off because the cork has, for some reason, perished.

CRU. Growth. A particular growth is described as a "Premier Cru", "Grand Cru" etc. . . . .

CUVÉE. Contents of a cellar.

DRY. Not sweet.

FINE CHAMPAGNE. Brandies from the Grande or Fine Champagne district. Not to be connected with champagne as such.

FIERY. Applied to raw spirits.

FRAPPÉ. Wines iced sufficiently for the table.

GREEN. Young immature wine.

MUST. The grape juice before it becomes wine by fermenting.

OEIL DE PERDRIX. (Partridge eye). Descriptive name given to the colour of some white wines—champagne, white burgundies.

PHYLLOXERA. An insect pest that destroys vines.

PROOF. The standard estimate of alcoholic strength of a spirit. In the U.K. proof spirit at 60 deg. F. contains 57.06% of absolute alcohol by volume. 49.24% by weight.

RACKING. Separating the bright wine from the deposit.

SEVE. Word generally employed to indicate the vinous strength and the aromatic savour which develops in the mouth at the time of tasting wine.

VIN ORDINAIRE. Poorer quality wines.

VINTAGE WINES. Wines of higher character, principally port, clarets, burgundies and sauternes shipped under their respective years.

WOODY. Wine tasting of wood because a stave in the cask may have started rotting—thus giving the wine an unpleasant flavour.

6

How to be an English-Wine Snob

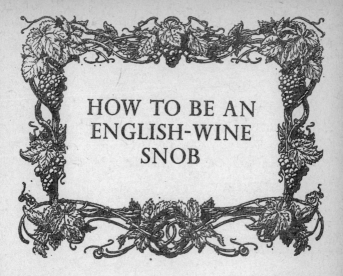

HOW TO BE AN ENGLISH-WINE SNOB

The English-Wine snob absolutely refuses to drink home-made wines. He may dabble in making the odd gallon of parsnip, or dandelion for a giggle, but he will never *be seen* drinking anything but the carefully manufactured, so to speak "Chateau bottled" wines.

The grape is of little interest to the English-Wine snob when he really gets down to it. What he enjoys is the wine made from the fruit this country produces so naturally and so abundantly. But it is essential to remember that continuity of quality is vital. The difference between home-made wines and manufactured wines is simply that the latter are always constant, always reliable and always available. Home-made wines are not.

Offering an English fruit wine can meet with some fear and trepidation from a guest. He has heard of Elderberry wine, Bilberry, Blackberry, and to him all fruit wines may be synonymous with old lace, with witches brews, with doubtful recipes, unpleasant looking fermentations, cloudy concoctions. To offer a home-made wine is similar to offering mushrooms which have only just been picked in the field beyond the garden—it does not help the guest feel comfortable.

On the other hand if you offer, let us say, one of the Merrydown English fruit wines, then you are offering a welcome gift. The guest is instantly re-assured. He has heard of Merrydown, and if he has not the labels and bottles themselves are pleasing enough for him to realize that he is not going to drink a medicine but a wine that other people have been drinking for some time.

If you aspire to be the perfect English-Wine snob, you must then know exactly how to serve each individual wine—for of the twelve that are on the market each is different and must be treated individually.

APPLE WINE

This, the first genuine apple wine to capture the attention of the public made its appearance in 1946 immediately after the war. Produced entirely from apples and sugar, it has taken its place among the wines of the world with which it effectively competes.

It should be served chilled, not iced.

In the summer it is ideal for a refreshing pre-luncheon drink and has the advantage of being palatable throughout any meal, blending both with fish and meat dishes.

If other wines are served during a meal, the apple wine should be kept till last.

It should be served in a clear, large, tulip shaped glass with stem, as for burgundies or indeed clarets.

Due to the fact that this wine was made from apples, some unfortunate unenlightened people believed it to be a type of cider and drank it by the pint in beer glasses. The results were unpleasant for everyone concerned and gave the wine a rather "rowdy" name in certain circles. Should you at any time, therefore, be offered a Merrydown Apple Wine in anything but a wine glass it is only proper that you should leave the company and your host as quickly as possible. Such people are not to be associated with.

BILBERRY WINE

The bilberry has other names—whortleberry, blueberry, blaeberry. The resulting wine is a clear red coloured liquid similar in taste to some Continental red wines. It can be served chilled, but is ideal at room temperature served throughout the meal. It is a dry wine and has characteristic astringency. It should be served in a similar way to that of apple wine and is the perfect partner for most meats, steak, grilled lamb cutlets, roasts.

BLACKBERRY WINE

This is a good drinking wine less suitable as an accompaniment to a meal than for pleasure-drinking.

It is a picnic wine, a wine to drink late at night, mulled in cold weather with lemon peel and nutmeg. The English-Wine snob seldom serves this wine for luncheon or dinner if he wishes to impress his guests, but it is a homely wine and one which he indulges in privately, much as he might indulge in a vin ordinare if he didn't prefer English vintages to French. It is a week-day wine, quite drinkable out of a tumbler. Thick glass, in fact, adds to the pleasure. A healthy drink, one that seems to replenish the blood.

ELDERBERRY WINE

This red wine has a distinctive flavour which blends well with meat. It should be served at room temperature in clear glass of the shallower tulip bowl design. Though it goes well with meat, it is also a vegetarian's wine complementing any simple vegetable dish. It is usual for the

English-Wine snob to decant elderberry wine and serve it from a thin glassed decanter, its colour gracing the table. Though its medicinal properties are well known—it is frequently prescribed to combat neuralgia and the common cold, containing magnesium, phosphorous, sulphur and iron,—the wine snob does not usually like to refer to it as a health cure. It stands on its own two feet as an excellent table wine without the aid of doctors.

GOOSEBERRY WINE

This is a medium dry wine and should be drunk at the beginning of a meal, chilled, and with fish. The stronger fish dishes should be eaten with it, not the more delicate. A lobster or oysters might suffer, but prawn cocktail, Sole Normande, grilled plaice or indeed a Bouillabaise will be enhanced by it. Though it could be served in tall stemmed green glasses, it would seem impertinent to the wine snob to do so. A simple, thin, clean bowl-glass should suffice.

MORELLO CHERRY WINE

This is an after-dinner wine, the port of fruit wines. A suspicion of almond flavour stimulates the appetite perhaps, but its place is after a good dinner with a cigar. Deep red, warm and comforting it helps the digestion and pleases the eye. It can, of course, be served as a sweet pre-luncheon drink and, in fact, is popular in France as an aperitif, but the wine snob knows that its place is at the end of a meal, not the beginning. It should be drunk out of an "old" glass, if possible an old cut glass. Small, deep, giving the imbiber a large tot rather than a small drink.

ORANGE WINE

This is a deceiving wine, quite clear, white, and gently reminiscent of the fruit it comes from except when tasted with a dish blended with oranges when the actual "fruit" taste is recalled. Prepared from bitter oranges only, it is a dry, very pleasant wine which the snob always drinks from miniature shallow champagne glass bowls. This glass is not small, but smaller than the average glass wrongly known as the champagne glass. Though served chilled, the bowl allows it to regain the room temperature slowly and this enhances its unique bouquet of orange blossom. The taste is quite different to its nose. It is an ideal wine to drink throughout the meal, but really should be kept for the game, meat or poultry. Canard a l'Orange is naturally a good choice as this brings out its special flavour.

Though the English-Wine snob might well suffer a traumatic experience when reading this I personally think it ideal for cocktails, laced with a little gin or vodka. This however should not be seen to be done if you wish to be respected by other English wine lovers.

RASPBERRY WINE

This is an after-roast wine, a deep, sweet wine to be drunk at the end of a good dinner party with the dessert. It is a dessert wine. Sweet, fruity, recalling the taste of raspberries very slightly, it is a good wine to start developing the palates of children to wine drinking—though not everyone agrees that this should be done. From the health point of view, however, wine is good for you, fruit wines are better and to deny children of over seven the pleasure of wine drinking, in small quantities of course and always with meals is, I personally think, a shame. Fruit wines are better than grape wines for children, raspberry wine, watered down, is an ideal starter. For those who like a really sweet cool drink in mid-afternoon, iced raspberry wine is extremely pleasant, though with a meal it should be served in a normal wine glass at room temperature. It can also be served from a thick cut glass decanter.

RED CURRANT WINE

Though red, this wine should be served chilled. It is a rose wine. Made with both red and black currants its colour is extremely pleasing to the eye, and its tang, reminiscent of gunflint, can be compared to many a good French vintage.

Unlike any other red wine, red currant wine is the only one which should be served in tall stemmed coloured glasses, preferably blue, and only if served at the very beginning of a meal. This tradition dates back from the time when the first experimental red currant wine was drunk by the makers who only had tall Moselle glasses to taste it in. The colour blend with blue glass and deeper red proved so pleasing to the eye that the wine snob who "knows" about its history continues this tradition.

When served with meat, however, red currant should not be chilled, but equal to room temperature and served in a rather deep bowl glass, clear not coloured.

RHUBARB WINE

A white wine which, like gooseberry, improves with age. Soon there will be notable vintage rhubarb wines and the discerning palate will make sure its gets the older ones. A useful everyday wine as well as a pleasant table wine which can be served, chilled, throughout the meal.

WHITE CURRANT WINE

Despite the fact that all these wines are remarkably inexpensive, all provide extreme pleasure. White currant wine, however, excels everything and should be treated with veneration. It is a clear white wine, dry, quite unique in flavour among fruit wines rivalling any Alsatian, Hock or Moselle. It should always be served chilled in tall stemmed glasses, coloured or not, and drunk with the most delicate of foods—smoked salmon, foie gras, oysters or caviare. It is the kind of wine made for wine tasting, ideal to savour, taste and re-taste. It is a favourite among English-Wine snobs when entertaining French-Wine snobs, for the French-Wine snob can never tell the difference and has, unfortunately for his own reputation, been known to praise it as "obviously a rare vintage from one of the steeper slopes of the Rhine."

To be an English-Wine snob, drinking English wines is not enough. He must have a reason to believe in them, he must be honest with himself and really prefer them to any other beverage. What then is so good about the wines of this country, how and why should anyone want to defend them in view of the fact that they seem to have been ignored for centuries?

It would be foolish to pretend that the production of fruit wines, which hitherto has been largely a matter for amateurs, can be regarded as an unqualified success. Triumphs by rural housewives have doubtless won fame— "Grandma's parsnip wine was a real blockbuster"—but how many gallons were poured down the sink as a result of complete failure?

It is hardly surprising that Grandma, with her chipped enamel saucepans, her methods of juice extraction generally involving the undesirable use of heat, her lumps of brewer's yeast floating on toast and her haphazard fining operation frequently created a concoction unlikely to appeal to discriminating palates. At the same time the foreign grape industry, with its elaborate and costly equipment, its State-subsidized assistance, its know-how through centuries of experience, its history alone, has enjoyed a huge advantage.

One must be realistic and not claim that wines made from other fruits are superior to those made by grapes, but

95

one can claim that some fruit wines are superior to some grape wines and that the majority of fruit wines now available in this country are greatly superior to the cheaper wines which are being imported and blended and sold under the name of Beaujolais or Vin Ordinaire.

The English-Wine snob has every right therefore to be proud of his label, if he wishes to wear it. He is the man who, when served a Spanish Burgundy, should sniff it with some distaste and enquire NOT why his host prefers it to a Chambertin—which would be ridiculous, but why he prefers it to a Merrydown Red Currant?

Why, when handed a glass of doubtful Graves he does not serve a white currant which is indeed far superior and far more palatable and, anyway, far cheaper?

The English-Wine snob, is a man who loves wine and is aware of what is best in certain circumstances. He may play with glasses and temperatures, he may serve English fruit wines at his best dinners, but if he is a true connoisseur, a gourmet, he will not, in fact, aim to be just a wine snob, he will try to be a wine lover.

If he can afford to serve Chateau Yquems, Chateau Lafites, Clos de Vougeots, etc. . . on certain occasions he may not be able to afford such wines *every* day, he may prefer to drink cheaper wines than none at all, and if he bothers to find out and experiment he will realize that, in the end he prefers to drink a bilberry wine regularly, than one of those doubtful wines that come under various labels from abroad.

If you are ashamed to serve the English fruit wine on the table then you should think very carefully of what label you are going to present your guests with instead. A French wine? What French wine? And at what price? A Spanish wine? An Empire wine? A Yugoslavian wine?

Tut, tut.

7

The Merrydown Story

THE MERRYDOWN STORY

It might have been a little book with a paper cover, selling in Germany for about a shilling, that was mainly responsible for an idea shaping in the mind of a young Englishman before the second World War. This little text book, highly technical, confirmed the belief that it might be possible to produce drinkable wines from a variety of fruits, which had previously been considered totally unsuitable for this purpose.

Fortified with such theoretical knowledge Jack Ward managed to persuade his friend and neighbour Ian Howie to co-operate in a few experiments. Results were encouraging, in spite of enforced dependence on equipment designed for operations of a more domestic nature. An apple wine, fortuitously sparkling, a red currant wine and another, quite superb, made from white currants, began to reveal promising possibilities.

Came the war and with it a tiresome check to the programme of research. Experiments conducted in prisoner of war camps tended to assume an even more makeshift nature!

The conclusion of hostilities provoked a tide in the affairs of Howie and Ward. With a third partner it was decided to hazard the commercial production of fruit wines with a capital of £100, no premises, a minimum of technical knowledge and only a limited experience of marketing. A company was formed, which took its name from a modest little cottage overlooking the valley below the Sussex village of Rotherfield.

All kinds of difficulties presented themselves immediately. Fruit wines cannot be made without sugar, and sugar was rationed. An application was made to the Ministry of Food for an allocation for manufacturing purposes. It was turned down. This kind of setback was not sufficient to deter Howie, who had just spent $3\frac{1}{2}$ years mastering the more formidable problems that confront a prisoner of war bent on escape. With shameless persistence and a bottle of white currant wine to prove that a start had been made before the war, he managed to procure a grant of ten hundredweight, ostensibly for further research.

It was decided to make red currant wine to start with. After apples, this fruit was known to be the most suitable for conversion into a fermented drink and Ward knew that considerable quantities had been marketed in Germany before the war.

Some kind of pressing equipment was essential and enquiries revealed the existence of a rustic cider press in Rotherfield village. The ancient timbers were duly assembled in the Merrydown garage, the press cloths were purified in the family bathroom, ten gallon glass carboys were assembled to receive the juice and all was ready for the delivery of the fruit.

The operations had their funny side. Such unorthodox activities near Tunbridge Wells appeared to cause a measure of consternation to the local Excise Officer. With what seemed to be a somewhat inappropriate Entry Book, he arrived with his wife and pretty daughter to witness the pressing of a modest ton of fruit. His official status did not preclude him from lending a hand with the press when politely requested.

Next on the list was a similar quantity (about 500 gallons) of apple wine which had to be made in the autumn. At this stage the partners were undecided about the exact nature of the end product they hoped to achieve. While the apple wine and red currant wine marketed on the Continent might serve as a model, it was not certain whether in this form they would appeal to the British public. Some adjustments might have to be made. They were.

It is perhaps interesting to note that fundamental decisions taken in the early days have not been materially changed.

At this stage, it became essential to think about premises. One thousand gallons of wine in small containers can take up a vast amount of room, and even a second hand Nissen hut with lines painted on the ground is scarcely enough to cope with the regulation "apartheid" policy of separating gardening tools from such alcohol as may be likely to attract Excise scrutiny.

Then the first stroke of luck. A property investment by the Howie family furnished an option to take over a derelict manor house which for some years had been utilized as a residential country hotel. The building had been gutted by fire four years previously and stood, a gaunt skeleton, amid a sea of masonry. This derelict mansion became the registered office of the company.

Inevitably the company was confronted with its second

series of headaches. The wine had matured and must be bottled for sale. In what and how?

In 1947 no firm manufacturing wine bottles would take on a new customer. It meant second-hand bottles or nothing for the Merrydown Wine Company, and this led to many hours of laborious scrubbing, with bottle washing machinery of the most primitive kind. Champagne bottles were the easiest to obtain; nobody wanted them. They were too heavy for ordinary purposes, and as the firm found to its cost, the most difficult bottles in the world to clean. Considerable Gallic endeavour had obviously been exercised in order to invent a glue for the labels which would withstand hours of immersion in the ice bucket. Unfortunately it proved equally impervious to the action of hot water.

Stability of the product after bottling proved an even greater problem. Certain wines, it seems, just will not settle down without special treatment; under the appropriate conditions they take on a new lease of life, with disastrous consequences if they happened to be sealed in a bottle. Ward and Howie learnt the hard way and their inexperience suffered embarrassing consequences.

The next problem was to sell what had been made. This proved to be considerably harder than initially expected. The national mistrust of anything new and unorthodox in the field of food and drink had been completely overlooked.

In order to get sales off the ground it was decided to market the apple wine as Vintage Cider. Familiarity with the national drink made from England's most popular fruit would serve to introduce the more sophisticated variety to the British public. In the case of wine made from red currant juice it was thought better to be frank with the customer. British Sherry as a title had provoked derision in certain quarters; Australian Burgundy was considered to be a misnomer in the worst possible taste; a futile deception therefore, by way of a misleading title, would, it was thought, do more harm than good. The directors of the company settled for Red Currant Wine and so it has remained ever since.

Wherever an outlet was achieved however, Merrydown Vintage Cider proved a winner and it became necessary to budget for increased production. The Ministry of Food increased its allocation of sugar from the ten hundred-weight to an annual quantity of five tons. Beyond this point it refused to budge in spite of repeated applications and visits by the importunate Howie.

The company therefore decided to explore the free market in sugar and found certain possible substitutes masquerading under innocent names such as Marsh-mallow Powder (sugar mixed with gelatine) Dutch Fondant (for icing cakes and confectionery) Apple Syrup from Australia (64% sugar, remainder water and apple essence supplied from England).

Such substitutes were expensive, involving dollar expenditure, with the result that Merrydown was required to pay over double the price for this essential raw material.

At the same time experiments were started at Horam Manor to discover whether it would be possible to obtain sugar from apples and these met with a certain measure of success. Fruit was considerably cheaper at that time and with the necessary machinery installed, it was established that this method of overcoming the supply problem might have been comparatively straight forward.

The immediate success of Merrydown meant additional staff. Initially however, sales and production were undertaken by the partners themselves. So also was the collection of bottles. Second-hand bottle merchants, off-licences, hotels, restaurants and even private houses were visited in order to collect the precious cargo of empty, often filthy, champagne bottles, assembled not infrequently in all kinds of dilapidated containers. These were immediately washed manually, and re-filled with vintage cider for delivery the following day to London and other parts of Southern England.

It soon became increasingly evident that such hand-to-mouth procedure could not be maintained for ever. Consignments of new champagne bottles were imported from France but matters came to a head in 1954, when it was found that the Merrydown product was being consumed in quantities greater than could be accomodated from the dwindling supplies of second-hand bottles available in Southern England. But conditions in the trade were gradually improving and by this time it was possible to find a firm ready to manufacture a special Merrydown bottle according to specifications.

During these formative years the premises were being slowly rebuilt. After cleaning mountains of mortar and brick rubble, scraping loose plaster off the walls, rubbing down charred woodwork with repeated hosing and sweeping, such delicate operations as filtering, bottle washing and sterile filling had somehow to be completed. There was no spare cash available for rebuilding, until some produce had been sold.

Two ground floor rooms in the derelict manor house were covered with a board and felt roof. Apart from this luxury, other parts of the building, including the cellars were exposed to the wind and the weather. In addition, funds were permitted to stretch as far as providing a couple of concrete floors. Occasional visits, made by directors and members of the staff to gleaming new factories erected for other industrial firms, provoked spontaneous envy and yearning.

With sales and profits increasing, it was possible to forge ahead with the programme of reconstruction and little by little the ancient manor house was restored, albeit with a new look. Additional outbuildings were necessary and as working conditions gradually improved, it became possible for the three partners to gain a measure of relief. Considerable financial restriction, aggravated by the necessity for providing expensive bottling machinery, vats, tanks and other storage containers, made the work of reconstruction seem painfully slow. It was some years before the directors could afford to draw a salary.

To-day, a visitor to the premises could hardly take in the extraordinary metamorphosis achieved in less than a quarter of a century. The firm can boast some of the most up to date bottling facilities in the country, the first modern vinegar plant to operate in the British Isles and the latest type of apple press, again the first of its kind to press fruit on this side of the channel.

The success of the Merrydown venture was established in the first ten years of the company's existence. By 1956 the British Government began to take fruit wines seriously and somewhat clumsily included apple wine in the existing excise duty structure. The top heavy tax burden effectively curbed the company's magnificent progress. But that is another story.

8

~~~~~~

Recipes

RECIPES

LONG DRINK RECIPES

COLD RUSTIC PUNCH

For 30 glasses.

Pour 3 bottles of Merrydown Red Currant Wine
$\frac{1}{2}$ bottle Noilly Prat Dry Vermouth
$\frac{1}{4}$ bottle Bacardi Rum
2 miniature bottles of Orange Curacao
   in a large punch bowl and stir well.
Leave for two hours, then stir again.
Just before serving add in a large block of ice.
Pour in
2 one-pint bottles of fizzy lemonade.

Decorate with cocktail cherries, pineapple chunks and a sliced orange, but do not put in the liquor of any of these fruits.

CATSPAW

Non-alcoholic. For 1 glass.
In a tall 'collins' glass mix:

    1 fluid oz. Martlet concentrated apple juice
    1 fluid oz. pineapple juice
    1 teaspoonful cherry syrup
    Add two cubes of ice. Top up with soda and stir.

ROSE COLLINS

For 1 glass.
In a tall 'collins' glass mix:

   2 fluid ozs. Merrydown Morello Cherry Wine
   1 fluid oz. Daquiri Rum
   Add two cubes of ice and top up with Bitter Lemon.

SMUGGLER'S HOT PUNCH

For 12 8-oz. glasses.

Pour: 1 bottle Merrydown Elderberry Wine
         ½ bottle Dark rum
            into a ¼ punch bowl
Add: 1 teaspoonful of powdered cinnamon
         1 lemon cut in thin slices.

Mix: then pour over 3 pints of boiling water.
Stir: then add a little grated nutmeg.

The punch should be kept warm on a hot plate but should not be made to simmer.

COCKTAILS

LE DRAGUEUR DE MINES (Medium)

    ⅓ Bourbon whisky
    ⅓ Merrydown Mead
    ⅓ Noilly Prat Dry

1 dash Angostura bitters
Stir and serve with orange peel.

LA VEGA (Dry)

½ Merrydown Gooseberry Wine
⅓ Vodka
⅙ Noilly Prat Dry
1 dash Orange wine
Stir and serve with silverskin onion.

LA MANCHE (Sweet)

½ Merrydown Red Currant Wine
⅙ Merrydown Morello Cherry Wine
⅓ Gin
Stir and serve with cocktail cherry.

DUBLINER

3 parts Merrydown Elderberry Wine
1 part White Rum.

MERRYDOWN HONEYMOONER

2 parts Brandy
1 part Merrydown Mead
Shake with ice.

MERRY DOWNER

3 parts Whisky
1 part Merrydown Orange Wine
Shake with ice.

HORAM SPECIAL

3 parts Merrydown Apple Wine
2 parts Vodka

1 part Merrydown Orange Wine
Dash of angostura bitters
Shake with ice.

EIDERDOWN

1 part Gin
4 parts Merrydown Apple Wine
Lemon zest.

SCARLET LADY

1 part Gin
3 parts Merrydown Red Currant Wine

MOCK ORANGE

1 part Gin
4 parts Merrydown Apple Wine
3 parts Merrydown Orange Wine.

NORMAN'S CONQUEST

1 part Brandy
3 parts Merrydown Mead
Serve with ice.

This is a reversal of Merrydown Honeymooner and less potent.

FRUIT BOMB

2 parts Merrydown Morello Cherry
2 parts Merrydown Orange Wine
2 parts Vodka
Lemon zest.

L'EAU D'ARUN

For ⅓ pint glass:
    ½ St Raphael Blanc
    ½ Merrydown Red Currant Wine
    Served on ice with a slice of Orange
    Top with soda.

THE TRUNDLE

    ⅖ Merrydown Elderberry Wine.
    ⅕ Calvados
    ⅖ Merrydown Bilberry Wine
    Served on ice with slice of cucumber
    Float a little Yellow Chartreuse on top.

GOODWOOD SILK

    ¼ Merrydown Rhubarb Wine
    ¼ Merrydown Red Currant Wine
    ¼ Merrydown Orange Wine
    ¼ Lemon juice
    Dash of white of egg
    Shake furiously in cocktail shaker
    Top up with soda and add sprig of mint.

WINE CUPS

PARADISE WINE CUP

Steep 1 lb of fresh strawberries, peaches or other fruit in
two bottles of Merrydown White Currant Wine (or
Medium Sweet Vintage Apple Wine) and two liqueur

glasses of Brandy for at least an hour before it is required.

Just before serving, add ice and sugar to taste, and finally one bottle of champagne or other sparkling wine.

The ingredients are best mixed in a large glass or china bowl and served with a ladle.

GOBLIN'S CUP

Mix, in a quart jug, with a little ice, one large wine-glass of gin, one large wine-glass of orange squash, half a bottle of Merrydown Vintage Apple Wine (Medium Sweet) and top it up with soda.

MERRY COBBLER

> 1 part Whisky
> 4 parts Vintage Apple Wine (Medium Sweet)
> 2 dashes Angostura bitters
> Top up with soda. Serve with ice and mint leaf.

ADAM'S DELIGHT

In a large glass jar place pieces of ice and add one liqueur glass of Calvados. One liqueur glass of cointreau or curacao. 1 liqueur glass of brandy.

Mix in two bottles of Merrydown Vintage Apple Wine (Medium, sweet or dry).

Garnish with borage or fruit in season and top up with soda.

JOUSTER'S REVIVER

Put a bottle of Merrydown Mead and a bottle of tonic water in the refrigerator twelve or so hours before you need them.

Mix two parts of Mead to every one part of tonic and serve with a slice of lemon.

JOUSTER'S SOOTHER

Blend 5 parts of Mead with 1 part of Dry Vermouth, serve with ice, a mint leaf and a slice of lemon.

ORANGE WINE CUP

In a bowl empty the contents of a tin of mandarin oranges. Add two bottles of Merrydown Orange Wine and 4 liqueur glasses of gin. Just before serving throw in a quantity of ice, a little sugar to taste and a bottle of Sparkling Cider.

MERRY RYE

In a bowl empty half a bottle of Merrydown Red Currant Wine. Add a glass of rye whisky, four glasses of Merrydown Vintage Apple Wine (medium sweet), a little maraschino and sugar to taste. Throw in some ice just before serving.

HAWAIIAN CUP

Mix 2 bottles of Merrydown Vintage Apple Wine (medium sweet) with 2½ pints of water. Pour in a quantity of pineapple chunks and orange slices. Strain, then add a liqueur glass of Kirsch, 3 glasses of Apple Wine. Shake with ice, serve with a strawberry in each glass.

TEENAGE CUP

Squeeze the juice out of three oranges. Dissolve two or three tablespoonsful of sugar in the juice. Add a bottle of Merrydown Vintage Apple Wine (medium sweet). Top up with soda water.

NANCY'S FANCY

Mix together a half bottle of Merrydown Vintage Apple Wine (medium sweet) and two tablespoonsful

115

of sugar with the juice of three oranges and one lemon

Just before serving add the whole contents of a soda syphon. Add ice cubes.

MERRYDOWN FRUIT CUP

Steep a pound of strawberries or other fruit in two bottles of Merrydown White Currant Wine and two liqueur glasses of brandy for at least an hour before required.

Before serving add ice and sugar to taste and finally one bottle of Champagne. Mix in a large bowl and serve with ladle.

HOT PUNCHES

HOT PUNCH

Put one teaspoonful of tea, four or five cloves, half teaspoon of powdered cinnamon and a little grated lemon peel into a large china or earthenware jug.

Pour on 1¾ pints of boiling water.

Stir the mixture and allow to draw for five minutes before straining into punch bowl.

Meanwhile heat, without boiling, a bottle of Merrydown Red Currant Wine—or Medium Sweet Vintage Apple Wine—with ½ lb sugar and ⅛th bottle of rum.

Add to the mixture in the punch bowl and serve piping hot.

ALPINE PUNCH

To 2 bottles of Merrydown Elderberry Wine add the juice and peel of four oranges, ⅛th oz. cloves (about 30) and ¼ oz. stick of cinnamon.

Allow to stand for 2 hours in a china, glass, enamelled or stainless steel jug before straining through muslin.

Heat gently—without boiling—in a saucepan, pour into a punch bowl and serve.

116

PLANTAGENET PUNCH

Mix together 8 parts Merrydown Mead
2 parts Port
1 part Brandy
2/3 sticks cinnamon.

Heat gently without boiling. If large quantity is required add more cinnamon.

MERRYDOWN HOT TODDY

Put 2 good tablespoonsful of honey in a saucepan (it is best to use clear honey). Add 1 bottle of Merrydown Vintage Apple Wine—or Red Currant Wine. Heat gently without boiling, add a small stick of cinnamon and the juice and rind of 1 lemon. Pour into a punch bowl, or a china or earthenware jug or bowl, and serve piping hot.

MERRYDOWN MAGIC

Gently heat, without boiling:
4 parts Merrydown Mead
2 parts Merrydown Elderberry Wine
1 part Vodka
Pour into punch bowl and serve hot.

CRUSADER'S FAREWELL

In a shaker mix:
Yolk of egg
2 parts Mead
1 part Dry Sherry
2 dashes Angostura bitters
Ice.

FRIAR'S HABIT

Mix well:

> 1 part Whisky
> 2 parts Sweet Vermouth
> 6 parts Mead.

This can be served chilled or hot.

BEOWULF'S WHISTLE

> 3 parts Mead
> 1 part Brandy
> ½ teaspoon Maraschino Syrup
> 1 Maraschino Cherry.

MINSTREL'S CALL

1 part Whisky
2 parts Ginger
4 parts Mead.
Shake with ice and add dashes of Angostura bitters
to taste.

DRUID'S DELIGHT

> 1 part Dry Vermouth
> 5 parts Mead.
> Serve with slice of lemon and mint leaf.

YOUR RECIPE
NOTES

NEL BESTSELLERS

F.1500	THE ADVENTURERS	Harold Robbins 10/6
F.1892	79 PARK AVENUE	Harold Robbins 7/6
F.2235	THE DREAM MERCHANTS	Harold Robbins 8/6
F.2082	WHERE LOVE HAS GONE	Harold Robbins 7/6
F.2084	THE CARPETBAGGERS	Harold Robbins 9/6
F.2096	SOMETHING OF VALUE	Robert Ruark 7/6
F.1532	A GREEN TREE IN GEDDE	Alan Sharpe 7/6
F.1485	LUST FOR LIFE	Irving Stone 6/-
F.1627	THE SHOOT	Elleston Trevor 5/-
F.1533	MESSIAH	Gore Vidal 5/-
F.1212	THE THREE SIRENS	Irving Wallace 7/6
F.2061	THE PRIZE	Irving Wallace 9/6
F.1323	FLOODTIDE	Frank Yerby 5/-
F.2098	CAPTAIN REBEL	Frank Yerby 5/-
F.2100	THE VIXENS	Frank Yerby 5/-
F.1406	FAIROAKS	Frank Yerby 5/-
F.1992	GILLIAN	Frank Yerby 5/-
F.2099	TREASURE OF PLEASANT VALLEY	Frank Yerby 5/-
F.1923	TO SIR WITH LOVE	E. R. Braithwaite 5/-
F.1615	THE HELLFIRE CLUB	Daniel P. Mannix 5/-
F.1596	A REED SHAKEN BY THE WIND	Gavin Maxwell 3/6

NEL P.O. BOX 11, FALMOUTH, CORNWALL

Please send cheque or postal order. Allow 6d. per book to cover
postage and packing (Overseas 9d. per book).

Name...

Address ....

....